*"As a successful organizing coach, I immediately related with Lo
concepts in The Clutter Diet. Applying these principles can change your life!"*

—Dorothy Breininger
President of Delphi Center for Organization, Dr. Phil Show expert and author of *Chicken Soup for the
Soul - Life Lessons for Organizing and Balancing Your World*

*"Finally! A diet that's guaranteed to work! Bite by bite, The Clutter Diet will move
you closer to your goals. It's a recipe for success – a smart, sensible plan that makes
it possible for anyone to get organized once and for all."*

—Donna Smallin
Author of *The One-Minute Organizer* and *A to Z Storage Solutions*

*"I can't think of anyone who wouldn't benefit from this book. Even the most orga-
nized people are looking for ways to be less cluttered and more effective, and those
of us who struggle to get and stay organized need the kind of real-life information
that Lorie Marrero offers. Mark Twain once said, 'Progress starts with the truth.'
This book offers the truth about your clutter and how you can eliminate it forever!"*

— Barbara Hemphill
CPO®, Author, *Taming the Paper Tiger* book series

*"Lorie is the absolute best at simplifying what might otherwise appear complex. She
has given me proven tools, resources and ideas that have helped me organize every
part of my life, saving me time, money and energy."*

—Lance Blanks
Cleveland Cavaliers Assistant General Manager

*"The Clutter Diet is a must-read for anyone wanting to get and stay organized.
Lorie's real-life examples and step-by-step strategies will have you thinking like an
organized person in no time. Get ready to accomplish great things!"*

—Audrey Thomas
CPO®, author of *50 Ways to Leave Your Clutter* and *The Road Called Chaos*

*"Lorie is an industry pioneer who tells it like it is and reveals all her secrets to ensure
your success. If you're serious about getting rid of the clutter in your life once and
for all, this book is the one you've been waiting for."*

—Barry J. Izsak
CPO®, CRTS, Author of *Organize Your Garage in No Time*
Immediate Past President, National Association of Professional Organizers

To Pete, the most supportive husband possible, and Susan, my longtime Motivation Partner and friend who gets all credit for starting me down this path in 2005.

The Clutter Diet®

The Skinny on Organizing Your Home and Taking Control of Your Life

Lorie Marrero

Certified Professional Organizer® and Creator of ClutterDiet.com

Reason
Press
Austin, Texas

Reason
Press

PO Box 40460
Austin, Texas 78704
512-498-9800
publisher@reasonpresspublishing.com

Edited by Lorraine Fisher
Cover and book design by Donna Coffelt (www.coffeltdesign.com)

First Edition
Library of Congress Control Number: 2008942726
ISBN 9780615266480

Section Images Copyright GoodMood Photo, Luxe, Svetlana Larina, Gordon
Swanson, and Asasirov 2008. Used under license from Shutterstock.com.

3 4 5 6 7 BP 14 13 12 11 10

Table of Contents

Chapter 8: Allowing Clutter

- The two kinds of "invisible clutter" you are allowing into your life without even realizing it!

Section Three: Reduction

Chapter 9: Losing Clutter-Pounds℠!

- Five ways to lose Clutter-Pounds
- How to make your own "Disposal Plan"

Chapter 10: Important SpaceScaping® Concepts

- The most common "diagnoses" for what ails your space
- How a three-letter Spanish word can help you be a better organizer

Chapter 11: How to Approach Your Projects

- Our basic O.R.D.E.R. approach that works for almost any organizing project
- Five ways to find hidden space
- How to choose containers for storage

Chapter 12: How to Get Organized to Do Organizing

- The essentials of an Organizing Toolkit
- Where to start and how to tackle your projects

Section Four: Maintenance

Chapter 13: The Foundation of Home Organization: Systems & Routines

- The three kinds of organizing that form the structure of your home
- How to successfully add new habits into your life

Chapter 14: Creating Your Morning and Evening Routines

- How to "just DEW it" with your morning "To D.E.W." list
- What "Triple S" means for your evening at home

Chapter 15: Creating Your Administration System

- Learn strategies for activities, events, financial tasks, purchasing, and errands

Table of Contents

Getting Started

Imagine... as you wake up in the morning in your warm bed, you rub your eyes and look around you. You have a lovely bedroom with the sun shining in that seems to welcome you to the new day. You walk to your closet, open the door, and sigh pleasantly at your beautifully arranged clothes and shoes. You easily choose an outfit because you can see exactly what you have. You walk into your clean kitchen (after making your bed!) and you quickly prepare a healthy meal for yourself and clean it up right away without thinking twice. Later that morning, the doorbell rings. It's your next-door neighbor stopping by... for a moment you panic! But then you realize there is nothing to fear. You spontaneously invite your neighbor in for coffee and enjoy a conversation free from worry about what she thinks about the condition of your house. When your neighbor leaves, you return to your personal projects and reflect in appreciation on the streamlined and comfortable environment you have achieved—one that motivates and supports you in your personal and professional goals.

Does this feel like an impossible dream?

Why does this all seem so hard? Well, it's not just you! Almost everyone is struggling with organization in this modern world. Simply stated, we have too much data, too much stuff, and not enough time to manage it all. Every day, we are flooded with a fire hose of information from e-mail messages, radio, television, the web, and even ads on the back of restroom doors.

Did you know that Americans can choose from more than 45,000 supermarket items[1], 386 kinds of cereal[2] and 22,652 magazines[3]? And you should see the array of salsa choices if you live in Texas! Even at times when we perceive our economy as down, we have an almost embarrassing abundance of riches. We have 24-hour stores, and when we buy something we are urged to "supersize" and "collect all four." We have, on average, much larger homes than ever before, but one out of 11 of us still rents a self-storage unit to hold our overflow of stuff. We need calendars for family activities, a task list, a soccer chair, a shopping list... and a nap. It's no wonder so many of us are struggling to keep up.

So how is getting organized like losing weight?

My team and I have told clients for years that the process of getting organized is very much like adopting a weight loss program. Why do we say this? There are many parallels and analogies—here are seven of the most compelling:

1. **Have you ever heard the expression, "A moment on the lips, a lifetime on the hips"?** Excess calories obviously result in an accumulation of fat on the body. The excess must be managed with exercise and reductions of caloric intake (eat less and move more). Clutter must be managed by preventing its entrance into

the home whenever possible and by regularly processing items and getting rid of what is not needed. Both weight loss and organization require a program of prevention, reduction, and regular maintenance.

2. **Crash dieting doesn't work, and neither does "crash organizing."** It's great if you tackle a few huge projects one weekend and get some areas really organized, but unless you change the habits that got you disorganized in the first place, you will soon find the space a mess again. Both weight loss and organization require working toward permanent changes in your habits and routines.

3. **Nobody else can make you go on a diet.** As Professional Organizers, we are asked all the time if we can "fix" our clients' spouses. Sometimes we are requested to organize a spouse's area when he or she is out of town. We don't do this for many reasons, but primarily because we cannot successfully organize a space for someone long term unless that person wants to make real changes for him or herself. Both weight loss and organization require a willingness to change on a personal level.

4. **Being overweight feels embarrassing and brings with it feelings of guilt, shame, and low self-esteem.** When you are disorganized, you feel out of control. You feel you can't have friends over, and you may get embarrassed by not showing up on time to appointments or keeping your promises to others. When people call us for help, we hear so many of the same feelings of frustration, stress, and guilt. Both weight loss and organization relieve embarrassment, reduce stress, and increase confidence.

5. **Support from a friend goes a long way.** Weight Watchers® figured it out a long time ago with their program that includes meetings. Having expectations to check in with your progress provides the accountability and support to keep you going. Both weight loss and organization are greatly improved with support and encouragement.

6. **Support from a trainer goes an even longer way.** For those who want more accountability and personal advice, hiring a personal

trainer is the sure-fire way to lose weight and get in shape quickly. Hiring a Professional Organizer in person is also the best way to get organized quickly and efficiently. Both weight loss and organization progress most rapidly with personal advice and accountability.

7. **People can have disorders related to clutter just like people can have eating disorders.** Some people may require assistance from trained professionals if they have hoarding disorders or other conditions causing a severe level of disorganization. Symptoms can include sanitation and infestation issues and a lack of basic functions of the home. If you need to learn more about severe clutter problems, visit www.nsgcd.org or call a mental health provider. Someone in this situation needs much more support to be successful.

Isn't it true that diets don't work?

When people say that diets don't work, they are usually talking about crash diets. Crash diets mean doing something drastic like fasting or drinking only carrot juice or special shakes, and then enjoying temporary results while you permanently mess up your body's metabolism. Crash diets are typical of our society's instant gratification mentality. Unless you change the habits that got you where you are today, you'll be right back where you started in no time. Diet programs that promote changes in your overall lifestyle are successful. Our Clutter Diet is not a crash diet, it's a permanent change in the way you see your time, your information and your "stuff." It works because it's not a temporary fix.

You may have tried to get organized many times before. Similar to weight loss, you may be a "yo-yo organizer." You may be burned out from trying, from "crash organizing" attempts that reverted back to chaos immediately. Why is this book different? Can this book really help you? Absolutely! First let me tell you a little about my background and how this book came about.

When I was ten years old, I saved up my allowance to buy a label maker, and I stayed in from recess to help other kids organize their desks. I have always had a passion for helping people save time so they can get more done! After college, I worked for a little while in Corporate America, and then my husband and I moved eleven times in about ten years. I definitely learned how to set up a household the most efficient way possible with two kids in tow. Along the way, we built four homes, and I learned many nuances about managing large projects and how a home is put together. We built some of our homes from scratch, starting only with some ideas and a drawing, and we brought those ideas into reality. We had to choose everything from the height of the doors to the color and type of the switch plates.

Since 2000 I have been organizing professionally, organizing everything from chemistry labs to backstage tour cases to ordinary closets. I have created massive filing systems with retention requirements lasting thirty years, and I have helped hundreds of people make their homes and lives work better.

As the owner of a service company with a team of Professional Organizers in Austin and San Antonio, Texas, I was bothered that so many people could not afford our hourly rates in person. I grew up in a family of school teachers, and we certainly could not have afforded to have someone come in to organize our closets. How could I reach people to help them affordably, from anywhere?

Eureka!

In January 2006 I had a "eureka" moment sitting on an airplane after attending an internet marketing seminar in Arizona. The whole weekend I had been saying to my friend, "I've got to figure out what the weight loss industry is doing. We're always saying that getting organized is a lot like losing weight! How could I help people the way they do?" I was staring out at the desert from the airplane window, and suddenly, it hit me! The Clutter Diet! I took out my notebook and feverishly wrote about 20 pages of how it would all work.

I jumped off the plane to catch the last leg of my flight home, and I whipped out my laptop to buy the domain for ClutterDiet.com. I knew this was the answer!

About a year later, our site launched, where we offer an affordable membership program that provides anyone access, from anywhere, to our team of organizing experts. We now have members from all over the world and an encouraging and supportive member community.

I realized that successful weight loss programs have figured out that it takes these *three key factors* to make personal change:

- **Motivation**—the "why" behind your goals and the tools to keep you on track
- **Education**—the "how" that provides good information, plans and advice
- **Support**—the help you need to get answers and encouragement

Our program helps people get organized by providing all three of these things for a low price, and we have a lot of fun with the diet metaphor. Members lose "Clutter-Pounds^{SM}" from their homes, and they "weigh in" to get our weekly "menu" plan of projects.

Why don't books always work?

I resisted writing a book for a long time, because I wanted to make sure that I had something important to say to people that was different. Also, our clients have often had a huge number of organizing books that we then, ironically, have to organize for them.

Sometimes people are quite successful at reading organizing or weight loss books and getting great results. But why don't books always work? Of the three key factors necessary to make change, books can educate and motivate, but books don't provide support. When is the last time one of your books jumped off the shelf and asked you how you were coming along?

Many organizing (and weight loss) books also do not provide enough coverage of motivational concepts. They spend a lot of time on the "how to do it" part, with great tips or recipes, and not enough time on "why." So I finally realized that I could write a book that would emphasize all three key factors.

You see, I believe that organizing itself is not difficult if you understand some basic concepts. Almost every single dieting book really boils down to "Eat Less, Move More." And almost every single organizing book boils down to "Keep and Do Less, Live More." These are not difficult ideas, but what makes success difficult for people is the psychology around doing it.

The root of all disorganization is truly delayed decisions and actions. Look around you—every bit of clutter on your kitchen countertop, your desk, or your coffee table is something that has not been decided yet or something that has not been done yet. In other words, *procrastination is the cause of almost all clutter.*

In summary, what people really need is to get unstuck. Once they get a little expert advice on HOW to do it, then what is really needed is the motivation and support for getting it done.

How This Book Works

One thing that makes this book different from others is our free companion workbook, downloadable at www.clutterdiet.com/book. There are no roadblocks set up to receive this download—no registrations or personal information are required. You can print this workbook out and use it as you read this book to make your own personal goals and plans. There is a Clutter Fitness Exercise section at the end of each chapter that makes this book interactive, brings the concepts to life in your own situation, and helps the concepts to stick.

We have divided the book into sections for Getting Motivated, Prevention, Reduction, and Maintenance. And just like a diet book, we're going to put all of the good recipes for the plan in the back of the book together in our *"Room by Room Recipes"* section, giving you our specific approach for the most commonly disorganized areas.

Here's how our easy plan is going to make your organizing journey successful:

Motivation:

- *Section One: Getting Motivated* contains information on getting the right mindset, and on procrastination, common barriers, and ways to break through them
- Helps you outline and identify your compelling "WHY" for getting organized
- Helps you outline and identify your own roadblocks getting in the way
- Helps you set up your support system to be successful

Education:

- *Section Two: Prevention* contains information on the three ways clutter enters your life and how to cut those "Clutter Calories"

- *Section Three: Reduction* contains instructions on how to lose accumulated Clutter-Pounds^{SM}, how to create your own disposal plan, and how to approach your organizing projects with our SpaceScaping® method

- *Section Four: Maintenance* tells you how to set up your basic household systems and keep them functioning

- *Section Five: Room by Room Recipes* covers specific areas like closets, bedrooms, and basements

Support:

- Our workbook's Clutter Fitness Exercises will help you set up your own personal support system for success

- If you like, you can sign up for our Clutter Diet program to get advice and support from our experts and our encouraging member community

Your First Clutter Fitness Exercise

Download the free companion Clutter Fitness Workbook at www.clutterdiet.com/book, print it out, and staple or clip it together. Again, no registration or personal information is required for the download. (The workbook is in Adobe PDF format. Get the free reader at Adobe.com if needed.) If you are really motivated and have a three-ring binder, you can punch holes in the pages and put it in the binder. Gather a highlighter and a pen to have with this book while you read it.

What you can do

is often simply a matter

of what you will do.

– **Norton Juster,**

The Phantom Tollbooth

Getting Motivated

How to Think Like an Organized Person

What does it even mean to "be organized?" Does it mean that you're on top of everything, that you never miss a beat, that your home looks like a magazine photo at all times? Does it mean that you're neat, regimented, perfect, and a minimalist? Does it mean that somehow magically you've gained the ability to "do it all?" Or does it mean that you are now (gasp)... *"PERFECT?"*

Let's start this diet by setting our expectations appropriately. We have to know what success looks like in order to achieve it. **Our definition of being organized is represented by the word "N.E.A.T.E.R."**

Not perfect - good enough!
Efficient - minimizing waste & effort
Always improving - making laziness work for us
True to your style - making it work for YOU
Effective - doing what works
Ready for anything - being prepared for life

Not perfect

Builders' model homes simultaneously attract and repel me, like a wax statue that you know is not real and yet you just can't help looking. They seem so lifelike... yet, there is something missing... oh, yes, it's people! Actual inhabitants and their actual stuff.

Home decorating magazines, advertisements, television show sets, and model homes have all given us an unrealistic ideal image of what our homes are supposed to be like. Your family's home is not going to look like a model home any more than you are going to magically look like Cindy Crawford.

Our ideal image of what our homes should look like is distorted by the popular media, in exactly the same way that women's body images have been distorted by airbrushed, unnaturally thin models. Rooms in magazine stories and advertisements are staged by teams of designers and stylists, just like models are made up by teams of makeup artists and hairstylists.

I am on a mission to make sure that homeowners everywhere do not think their homes are supposed to look like that! We *live* in our homes... they are not museums. I have been featured in these magazines and work with their editors frequently, and I understand why they need to make their photos look this way. I am not saying at all that you shouldn't read these magazines; I simply want people to be educated about what has gone into preparation for these photos and see them with a trained eye.

"Good Enough" is good enough! Perfection is an unattainable goal... an illusion. And perfectionism is one of the major causes of procrastination. "If I can't do it right, I don't want to do it at all." Doing it 80% right is better than doing 100% of nothing at all! Give up on "perfect" TODAY.

Efficient

Being efficient means doing things with minimum waste of time and effort. Carpooling is one of the best examples of efficiency. You're already going there, and I am already going there, so let's go there together, saving time, energy, and money!

If you have several tasks to do, think first of the one that could be simultaneously running while others are being done. For example, you can start the laundry first before straightening the kitchen, since the washing machine and dryer can be running without you. You can put dinner in a slow cooker first while you go about your day.

Being efficient means you are continually conscious of your processes for doing things. And that leads us to our next point, about improving these processes...

Always improving

People often ask me how I find out about this-or-that resource. I am constantly and actively looking for ways to make things work better. Essentially, I am organized because I am LAZY! I don't want to do things over again, waste time looking for things, or go out when I don't need to leave my chair. Almost every shortcut or tip I have found is a result of a passionate desire to not do things "the hard way."

Relentlessly ask yourself these questions
- How can I use my time better?
- How will I remember this later?
- How can I do this faster?
- How can I not do this at all?

Let's put our laziness to work by exploring each of these questions briefly:

How can I use my time better?
Focus on one thing at a time whenever possible. You might think of an organized person as juggling many things at once, but actually it's been proven more efficient to handle things one at a time. A recent *Wall Street Journal* article discussed how managing two important mental tasks at once reduces the brainpower available for either task. So, while people think they are saving time by multitasking, they are actually doing both tasks ineffectively.

But it is also true that you can walk and chew gum at the same time. Sometimes your activities do not require much brainpower, and multitasking does make a lot of sense. Here are some examples of great "no-brainer" multitasking activities:

- Talking on the phone while folding clothes or cleaning
- Listening to an audio book while cleaning, driving, or exercising
- Watching television while exercising
- Sorting mail while on hold

Waiting is almost always wasted time, unless you are prepared. Try to prevent this wasted time by going to places when they are less busy, such as shopping at off-peak hours.

If you know you are going to wait somewhere, you can bring things with you to do while you wait. Even if all you do is bring your own reading material, it is so much better to read your own things instead of the two-year-old parenting magazines they have at the doctor's office.

How will I remember this later?

When you know you'll need prompting on something at a later time, cue yourself in ways you can't miss, such as the way some people put their keys in the refrigerator with their lunch so they can't possibly forget to bring their lunch again! Try to outsmart yourself.

Don't reinvent the wheel. If you do something once, chances are you may need to do it again. Write it down and leave yourself a "crumb trail." Capture it into a trusted system, such as your computer, your calendar, or your filing system, so you can let that information go from your own brain and move on to other things. Here are some examples of capturing information:

- Keep driving directions to someone's house in your filing system or save them to a folder on your hard drive. You may want to drive there again.

- Open a word processing document or take out a legal pad to capture steps as you learn them, such as how to run a backup, how to download pictures from your camera, or how to set a clock on your electronic equipment.

- Write down birthdays in a "perpetual" birthday calendar as soon as you find out about them. (Get a free birthday calendar spreadsheet on our Free Tips page on our website at http://www.clutterdiet.com/freetips. Click on "Greeting Card Calendar Tool.")

- Make a note of phone numbers if you look them up even once. You can even make a label to stick on right where you need a specific phone number, such as putting the cable company's number right on your cable box for next time you have reception problems.

- Capture passwords and account numbers in one secure location.

- If you modify a recipe, write in pencil the changes you made to amounts or other instructions, so if the dish turns out better, you'll know what you did!

How can I do this faster?

Focus on saving steps. For example, if you are going upstairs, bring something up there that you already needed to put away. Busboys in restaurants save steps by using a plastic tub to gather dishes and take them to be washed. If you are going to run one errand, stop and think if there are others on your route you could do at the same time. Make sure you have everything you need with you, and ask everyone in the family if they need anything else before you leave.

How can I not do this at all?

Cross tasks off your list with these four techniques:

- **Prevent:** stop tasks before they start. Don't buy things that require a lot of upkeep or will be delicate to handle. Remember, everything you own is something you need to maintain. Buy more dark-colored clothing for children to camouflage stains, and don't buy white furniture or carpet.

- **Eliminate:** just stop doing it, if possible. What is the worst that will happen if you don't? Are you doing this task for perfectionist reasons? Are your standards too high? Do you really need to make the pie from scratch, or could you just buy one?

- **Delegate:** assign someone to do it for you. Enlist family members to help with things like house cleaning, lunch packing, dishes, grocery shopping, gift purchasing, and laundry. If you don't ask for help, it's not likely to appear.

- **Outsource:** pay someone to do it for you, as it makes sense for your budget. Don't forget to consider the cost of your own time in the calculation. Tasks like oil changes, housekeeping, and lawn care are time-consuming things that many people can afford to outsource. Hiring your friendly neighborhood teenager is one way to get these things done even more affordably.

True to your style

Release yourself from the trap of comparing yourself to how others' homes look and how other people think. Create your home environment around what you like, how your brain works, and how you are comfortable living.

Some people are really creative, and others are very logical. Some people like to see things out and around them, others like everything put away inside cabinets. Some are abstract thinkers, able to remember and envision a file tucked away in a drawer. Some are concrete thinkers, and that same file would disappear from consciousness and be "out of sight, out of mind." If you are an artist, your home is not going to look and feel like the home of someone who is an accountant. Honor yourself and your preferences, because that is the only way to create systems that work long term!

Effective

We've got to do what *works*. If your child goes into a phase of wanting peanut butter and jelly sandwiches for lunch every single day, it may be best to go with it, at least for the short-term, and simplify things for yourself. Why fight it? If something you do to stay organized works for you and your family, and everyone is still happy and healthy as a result, by all means, keep doing that. Don't let something you read here or in a magazine change what is effective for you.

I once spoke to a single man who lived in a small apartment with minimal kitchen cabinet space. He simply stored all of his everyday dishes in the dishwasher and ran it every night, clean or dirty! He fixed the storage problem and also kept himself from having to put all of the dishes away after washing. It was a very "bachelor" kind of solution, but it *worked*. Do whatever produces the intended effect!

Ready for anything

Being organized means being prepared for whatever life throws your way.
Need a fire extinguisher? Got one right here, step aside! Kids ready for
school the next day? Backpacks are at the door. Cut your finger? Get the
first aid kit!

When you have anticipated and planned, and you have systems that support
you in reminding you of tasks and purchases, you arm yourself against running out of things and being unprepared. Being organized means that you
and your family have what they need when they need it.

Being N.E.A.T.E.R. means that you have your act together, but you don't
live in a perfect model home dollhouse! It's a realistic definition of a goal we
can work toward.

Not perfect - good enough!
Efficient - minimizing waste & effort
Always improving - making laziness work for us
True to your style - making it work for YOU
Effective - doing what works
Ready for anything - being prepared for life

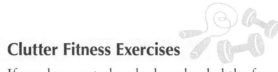

Clutter Fitness Exercises

If you have not already downloaded the free companion Clutter Fitness Workbook, print it out from www.clutterdiet.com/book.

- To reinforce them in your mind, copy down in your workbook the four questions that organized people ask themselves:
  - How can I use my time better?
  - How will I remember this later?
  - How can I do this faster?
  - How can I not do this at all?

Additional thoughts to explore:

- What is your own personal definition of what it means to be organized? What does being organized "look like" to you?

- What are 3 tasks you can cross off your list right now, whether from delegating them, outsourcing them, or eliminating them?

- What is one process you could improve in your house right now to save steps and other inefficiencies?

- What is one set of information you could capture that would save you having to "reinvent the wheel?"

I am convinced that
a calm, quiet and
harmonious interior can
be as beneficial to health
as a sensible diet and
regular exercise.

– Kelly Hoppen,

**British interior
designer and author**

Getting Motivated Is About YOU

Now that we have more clearly defined what getting organized really means, and you've started to change the way you look at the processes in your home, let's talk about where your motivation will come from to accomplish your goals.

Everyone is looking for a quick fix... the diet industry is rich with examples. Take this pill! Drink green tea! Get this surgery! I want to be honest about what I have seen as a consultant for these many years. What follows are some truths about this process that can be difficult to hear, but understanding them is necessary to make lasting personal change.

Truth #1: *You've always had the power!*

After her long adventure, when Dorothy finally learns how to go home at the end of *The Wizard of Oz*, she is told that she has always had the power to go back to Kansas. All she had to do was just click her heels together! Getting organized might not be as easy as clicking your heels, but you have always had the power to get it done. And while you can certainly utilize them as tools, no book, expert, or plan can get you organized in a permanent way—it's about making personal change in yourself and recognizing that the power to change resides within you right now.

Books and plans and experts like me are all external authorities, which are extremely helpful, but **your own internal authority is where the real power lies.** Trust yourself to know what is right for you.

Truth #2: *The state of your home is a reflection of your inner self.*

If your home is in a state of disarray, this particular truth may be difficult to hear. Your state of mind is reflected in the condition of your home, and you can consider it a mirror that gives you a lot of information about yourself.

Some of our clients have suffered from depression. When depressed, people tend to let go of things that don't seem to matter. Laundry and dishes may pile up, mail may go unsorted and unread, and bills may go unpaid. It becomes a chicken and egg question: Did the depression cause the clutter, or did the clutter cause the depression? We believe that each contributes to the other.

We shape our buildings, and afterwards our buildings shape us.

– Winston Churchill

There's only one way to solve this: Lose the clutter and reduce your stress. Find out what kind of person you can become by aligning your home to the life you want to have!

We firmly believe in getting support to make personal change, and we offer that support in our online member community. You can also create your own support network, and we will be guiding you in how to do that. But you may need more support than that… you may find that you need to visit a counselor in addition to following our plans if there are other related issues that are causing you to neglect your surroundings.

Truth #3: *You'll make personal changes in your life only if something is important to you.*

Your reasons for making changes must be compelling, but they may not be logical. Consider the smoker who knows the medical reasons for quitting, but he actually quits because his sweetie doesn't want to kiss him anymore. His reason is emotional, but it works for him.

Here are some common compelling reasons for getting organized:

- **You need to reduce your stress.** The Centers for Disease Control and Prevention state unequivocally that 80% of our medical expenditures are now stress related. You realize that the stress of your disorganization is something that must change.

- **You're embarrassed about the clutter.** Your biggest nightmare is someone dropping by unexpectedly. You don't feel comfortable having guests, and maybe your kids don't want to have friends over.

- **You want more time with your family.** The time you're wasting looking for lost items and catching up with wild goose chases is taking time away from the things that really matter to you.

- **You want to teach good habits and skills to your children.** You understand that you are a living role model whom your children are observing every day. For their sakes, you want to show them what good habits and systems look like.

- **You have a deadline.** You are imminently facing a big change like a move, a new baby, or a promotion which means you need to get things in shape quickly.

- **The clutter is holding you back from your goals.** You want to go back to school, change careers, or move, but your home environment does not support your being able to undertake the new challenges.

Truth #4: *Getting organized takes some time and energy.*

Despite an April Fool's blog post I once wrote about an "Organizing Magic Wand" now being available, unfortunately that was not real. Getting organized is just like any other goal—it's going to take some time and energy to get it done. Rome wasn't built in a day, and if you have years of accumulated belongings, it's going to take some time to get through them. The good news is that you will now have the motivation, education, and support to get that done!

If you decide to join our online program, you'll be able to follow our weekly project plans to work at least one hour on our main project (the "Main Dish"), 15 minutes on our two smaller projects (the "Side Dishes"), and five minutes on our little tip or task (the "Sensible Snack"), totaling less than two hours per week.

Your projects may seem overwhelming when considered as a whole, but breaking them down into manageable pieces will make them all possible. You've probably heard this joke before: "How do you eat an elephant?" "One bite at a time." You *can* eat that elephant! How do you think I wrote this book? Not all in one weekend!

Truth #5: *"The answer" does not come from a product or a tip or even a book like this.*

"The answer" to getting organized is about getting to the root cause of the issue and creating a system that works. People often rush off to their favorite discount store and start buying lots of bins, or they find a really nifty product that seems like it will solve everything. Products can be great tools, but it's not the product that truly solves anything. It's the methods and systems around the product. Even a simple product like a trash can is worthless unless you have a system of always throwing your trash into it and emptying it when full.

And tips are just tips. They are helpful and are good ways to be reminded of your goals and find out about new resources, but they are no substitute for going through the process of creating systems for you and your family. They are not a shortcut.

This book will provide you with guidelines and direction, but just reading this book is not a shortcut either. There is a huge difference between reading this book and applying the principles. Doing the exercises at the end of each chapter is VERY IMPORTANT. Actively participating in this book's program will reinforce your learning and help you carve out a plan for your own personal goals. And speaking of that, here are your next exercises:

Clutter Fitness Exercises

- What are your reasons for getting organized? Are they compelling? Write your top 3 reasons in your companion Clutter Fitness Workbook.

- Fill in the blanks:

  ○ If only I were more organized, I could _____.

  ○ If only I were more organized, I would feel _____.

  ○ If only I were more organized, _____ would be solved!

Ten Common Motivational Barriers

Staying motivated when making personal change is a journey, and as with any journey there are obstacles to overcome. Here are the ten most common obstacles that we see:

Motivational Barrier #1: *Procrastination*

As I stated earlier, delayed decisions and actions are at the root of all disorganization. Time management and clutter issues are therefore directly related to procrastination.

People often want to focus on WHY they are procrastinating. Entire books have been written to try to understand your "procrastination style" and analyze why you are doing it. Psychologist Dr. Linda Sapadin wrote *It's About Time: The 6 Styles of Procrastination and How to Overcome Them.* If you are interested in exploring whether you are a Perfectionist, a Defier, a Crisis-Maker or one of the other styles, this book is an excellent and in-depth examination of these ideas.

In my experience, however, focusing on the why is interesting but is not nearly as productive as focusing on how to solve it. We know that motivation and support are crucial to making personal change, and I have found it's extremely effective to focus on how to get that motivation and support to conquer the procrastination.

I really believe I know the cure for procrastination! It's called a "Motivation Partner." I have had a Motivation Partner for years—I have actually called her my "Accountability Partner," so you can decide which title resonates best with you. My friend Susan and I have provided this support to each other since 2001. We have a set day and time each week that we talk on the phone to discuss the following:

- What's going on
- What we each accomplished last week
- What we each are committing to doing this week

We have since added another partner, Audrey, and now the three of us talk each week for one hour. We are in completely different areas of the country— east, north, and south—but it doesn't matter. I can honestly tell you I would not have written this book without their support and accountability. I owe them chapters right now as I am writing this sentence!

For each thing we commit to doing we can choose to give ourselves either a consequence or a reward. Most often the consequence is simply the threat of embarrassment of having to answer to the other partners! We have also given ourselves rewards like a favorite bottle of wine, or consequences like not being "allowed" to attend an event. *Only you know whether a consequence or a reward would be more motivating for you*, and it will vary between different kinds of tasks. Here are some ideas for consequences and rewards:

Consequences or "Punishments"	Rewards
Getting up extra early for a few days	Going to a new movie or play
Not getting the reward you wanted	Buying something you've been wanting
Paying money to a political cause you hate	Eating at a favorite restaurant
Not being able to do something you like	Getting a special spa treatment
Facing the natural consequences that ensue	Spending time with a friend

The idea is that we often procrastinate because we don't have to answer to anyone but ourselves. Whether you do that because of perfectionism or because you are rebellious by nature… it doesn't matter. The accountability of a Motivation Partner is one of the most effective cures for procrastination I have ever witnessed.

According to the American Society of Training and Development, the probability of completing a goal is:

10% if you hear an idea

25% if you consciously decide to adopt it

40% if you decide when you will do it

50% if you plan how you will do it

65% if you commit to someone else you will do it

95% if you have a specific accountability appointment with the person to whom you committed

You can implement this as much as you need, even daily. I had a client, "Sharon," who was suffering from depression and some chronic illnesses. We worked together extensively, and Sharon went through a difficult time when she was having trouble with basic daily functions. One day we made an appointment for me to call her from my office to make sure she had taken a shower. This type of call was not a normal one for me to arrange, but for this person at this time, it was a lifesaver. Sharon reported that the only way she got herself up and around that day was knowing that I was going to call and ask. The accountability of another person's attention is incredibly powerful!

You can check in by phone, as my group does, and also via e-mail. You can report weekly or daily or as often as you like. I would not recommend doing this in person, however, as you may have a tendency to have longer meetings than necessary. Have a meeting occasionally in person as a reward for each other!

Why does this reporting work so well? A Motivation Partner forces you to create a deadline for yourself and provides the pressure that forces action. Most people work quite effectively with deadlines. That is why taxes are due in the US on April 15th, not "whenever you feel like it!"

Alternative ways to create a deadline:

- **Create "Public Declarations." On our Clutter Diet message boards we have a forum by this name.** Members use this section of the message boards to declare openly that they will do something they have been procrastinating and set a deadline for themselves. They additionally have the option of uploading a "before" photo of the space and getting our expert advice on what approaches, methods, and products might work well.

- **Write a blog about what you're doing.** One of our Clutter Diet members felt like it was not enough to be accountable to our message board community—she wanted to be accountable to the whole world! She wrote a blog about her projects with photos to embarrass herself into action. This is admittedly an extreme method, but it worked for her.

- **Have a party or other event in your home.** It's classic—once you know people are coming over, you must straighten things up, and it's incredibly motivating! You can create this deadline anytime you like and invite anyone you want. I will confess that my house has never been cleaner than when a TV crew is coming over to film! And our dinner parties and barbecues force us to scrub our patio furniture and do other seasonal or annual chores.

And finally, with regard to procrastination, our next chapter is entirely on overcoming the obstacle of just getting started. So often once you simply START a project, working on it actually becomes fun or at least pleasantly satisfying. We will be providing you several different ways of kicking yourself in the pants to get going!

Motivational Barrier #2: *All or Nothing Thinking*

Have you ever gone on a weight loss diet and followed "the rules" to the letter for several days, and then when you cheat by eating a dessert you feel like such a failure that you go off the diet completely?

First of all, you set yourself up for failure if you think that any human being could ever follow a program of any kind perfectly. Perfection is not realistic. Any program you follow should allow for exceptions and "real life."

You don't have to be either completely on or completely off a program, whether it's a weight loss diet or an organizational program. There will be days when you eat the donuts. But remember that there is such a thing as "Good Enough."

Just do the best you can every day and make sure that you are always trending toward improvement. If you look at a line graph showing the revenue of a healthy, steadily growing business, it shows some months are up and some months are down, but in general, the graph leans upward and to the right, and the trend shows *improvement over time*. Imagine if a business owner had a down month and said, "That's it, I am quitting!" As ridiculous as that seems, that is what we have done to ourselves when we fall in the trap of "All or Nothing Thinking."

Be forgiving of yourself, get right back on the horse and keep moving FORWARD.

Motivational Barrier #3: *Defeatist Language*

Our words define us. Words start as thoughts, and whether we say them aloud or just say them to ourselves, they begin to form our destiny. I am not sure if there is a way for me to emphasize this enough in written form! Can you imagine that I am grabbing you by the shoulders and insisting that you understand this part of the book? It's that important, not just for organizing, but for life!

> Watch your thoughts, for they become words.
> Watch your words, for they become actions.
> Watch your actions, for they become habits.
> Watch your habits, for they become character.
> Watch your character, for it becomes your destiny.
> **–Author Unknown**

Do you say things like this?

- "I am not a very organized person."

- "I will never get this mess cleaned up."

- "I'm such an idiot."

- "This mess is killing me."

- "I'll never get the hang of this."

Even if you think you are just kidding or exaggerating, DON'T communicate these negative and victimizing messages to yourself. All of your actions and habits start with thoughts and words. Be very careful! Ask yourself, "Would I say those same things to my best friend or my child?" If not, then why would you say them to yourself? Be kind!

Negativity in your words may also emerge in more subtle ways. Take care that you're not using permanent language for a temporary problem. If you say "I'm not very organized," you have assigned a permanent, unchangeable characteristic to yourself. The "All or Nothing Thinking" we talked about before also shows up in words like "never" and "always." Catch yourself and replace negative and permanent words with language that shows hope and belief in yourself and your abilities.

Here are some positive ways to rephrase these discouraging messages:

INSTEAD OF THIS...	POSITIVELY PHRASE IT THIS WAY INSTEAD:
Never	Sometimes, Rarely, Seldom, Barely, Hardly
Always	Sometimes, Usually, Frequently, Typically, Often
"I am not a very organized person."	"I am working on my organizing skills."
"I will never get this mess cleaned up."	"I will need to keep working on this for a while to get it done. I can do this."
"This is just how I am."	"I tend to approach things this way. How can I improve that?"
"I'm such an idiot."	"I made a mistake. What did I learn from it?"
"This mess is killing me."	"I am overwhelmed by this mess right now. What is one small step I can take toward fixing it?"
"I'll never get the hang of this."	"I am frustrated! How can I get some help?"
"I never remember to pay my bills."	"I sometimes forget to pay my bills. What can I do to help myself remember this?"

Motivational Barrier #4: *Physical Discomfort*

Our next motivational barrier can be summed up in one word: "EWWW!"
A project might involve being hot, dirty, smelly, dusty, icky, or just plain
unpleasant. Or all of the above!

We have organized in sweaty, sticky garages with mouse and rat droppings
all around us. And we have dealt with homes that have mold growing from
out of the vents in the wall, apartments that reek from dog urine and ciga-
rette smoke, townhomes that housed twelve cats, and garage projects where
we found ourselves outside in the rain dragging items back inside for cover.
One of my colleagues has even evicted a raccoon who was burrowed into
a mattress.

Here are some strategies for dealing with these conditions:

- **Do you have to do it right now?** Wait for a different time of year
  if possible. Don't try to organize an attic in August in Texas! The
  weather can make all the difference.

- **Ideally you should enlist someone to help you with extremely unpleasant situations.** Nobody wants to do this kind of work alone! Hiring a college student or a professional organizer, or getting a friend or family member to help you is key.

- **Equip yourself with any comfort options that are available.** Bring in equipment like a fan or space heater to make you more comfortable. Remember to stay hydrated and take more frequent breaks.

- **Gear up.** Physically prepare yourself for it by wearing gloves, a hat, a mask, or whatever is required to make you feel better. Gloves are often a must in garage projects. You may also need some cleaning products and tools like brooms, vacuum cleaners, and rags to clean the space as you go.

Motivational Barrier #5: *Emotionally-Charged Clutter*

Occasionally a project will involve some very strong emotional barriers. You might feel that you just can't bear to face the items. A death, divorce, or estrangement can make it particularly difficult to handle certain objects, especially photographs and memorabilia.

It's really important not to do this work alone if at all possible. It is easy to slip into the time trap of reading old letters, sinking into a chair with a stack of photos, or letting your emotions overtake you. A trusted friend will help keep you on track, preferably someone who does not have the same emotional hooks as you have in the situation.

If you can, get someone to "pre-sort" the items so you can just review them. Imagine the difference in approaching a room full of jumbled inherited items from a family member, versus approaching a room full of sorted piles of photos, jewelry, clothing, kitchen items, and other categorized items. Remember that organizing is very much about decision-making, and having sorted groups makes those decisions much easier.

We were once hired by a family to organize the home of their parents who had both died within months of each other. It was so much easier for us to sort things, especially since there was a lot of trash involved in this particular project and we were "separating the wheat from the chaff." The family was so grateful because we had staged a room for all of the requested items of the family members so they could come in and easily take the special paintings and furniture and other mementos that they wanted.

For more easily sorting these requested items, one of my colleagues made me aware that there are now different colors of painters' tape available at the hardware store. Painters' tape has traditionally been bright blue, and it has a lightweight adhesive for use in masking off areas to paint, so that it's easily removable and doesn't damage surfaces. Contractors often use this tape to mark things that need attention or repair. You can get these different colors of tape and assign a color to each family member, using it to mark and identify items that are reserved for them to have.

Know that it may take much more time to tackle these minefields of feelings than regular organizing projects. Remind yourself that this is normal and okay, and give yourself the time you need. However, if you do have a friend helping you, he or she can gently remind you to move along when you get stuck.

Don't let emotions like grief or guilt bully you into keeping things you don't really need in your life. Inherited items can come with feelings of guilt and obligation attached. Keep only a few strong sentimental reminders that are the most special of all, and constantly think about what you truly need and will use, rather than what you feel you "should" keep.

Motivational Barrier #6: *Ownership, or Lack Thereof*

"It's someone else's mess!" Does this sound familiar? When you share a home with others, your best efforts can often be foiled by the habits of children or spouses.

If I had the absolute answer to this problem I would be enshrined on Mount Rushmore! I know from experience that teenage boys can be the worst culprits. Sometimes these are problems that can only be managed, not really solved.

With other adults, start by using your best communication skills so that the other person takes at least partial responsibility for the problem. Fight fair, don't raise your voice, and talk earnestly about how it affects you and how you feel about the problem. Having this kind of discussion alone won't always work, but you'll have much more information after doing it that might help you change your approach.

You can also barter with adult "clutter culprits" to work on an area that is clearly important to you but not to them. Maybe there is something in that same category that the person wishes you would do differently.

You may possibly be able to negotiate that certain shared areas be maintained as clutter-free, while allowing that person his or her own areas. In those, you agree to give up control and let them keep them however they wish. I know a Professional Organizer whose spouse keeps a very messy desk and the couple compromises by saying "that space is yours, and this space is mine." You might want to stipulate, however, that the person maintains basic sanitation. It would not be acceptable to have a pest problem from food and dishes left in the area.

With children and teens, it's our responsibility as parents or adult role models to involve them in the process and teach them in an age appropriate way how to prevent the problem from happening again. Teaching them organizing skills is the more academic part of this problem. It's not terribly difficult to teach them the concepts involved. In reality it's mainly about these factors instead:

- **Importance:** People will take care of what is important to them, ultimately. My kids don't love school and particularly do not like certain teachers, and they just don't care as much about keeping their papers neatly together because it's not as important to them as other activities in their lives. I, on the other hand, really liked school at that age and it was important to me to do well and keep my stuff together.

- **Ownership:** It's simply not their house. I remember growing up that my room was certainly not as neat as I keep my room now. For example, I don't leave clothes on the floor now like I did then. When I got my own dorm room and shortly afterward an apartment, my neater habits kicked in. It was OWNERSHIP. It was *my space* and there was nobody else who was going to pick it up but me. My mom was not one to clean up after us that much per se, but there still was the latent sense of things when living at home that it was my parents' house and I was not ultimately responsible for it. My mother was typically the driver and initiator for whatever efforts were going to be made.

- **Perspective:** We understand why we need to turn the lights off because we pay the electric bills. We understand that if food is left around that it might attract pests, and we have the life experience to know how persistent and distasteful a problem that can be. We simply have a very different perspective from what our children can possibly have.

- **Congruence:** Kids are very observant. Are you being congruent with how you behave vs. what you are telling them? Do you leave clothing on the floor and then tell them not to? Practicing what you preach is important with kids of any age, but the teen years are when they are likely to throw it right back in your face!

- **Consistency:** Are you setting clear expectations and consistently following through with consequences when the expectations are not met? Remember, you're the one with the perspective and ownership in this situation, and it's up to you to maintain the standards that you want by following up until it's done.

As parents, we have to accept that, given the factors above, it's simply never going to be done as well as we might do it ourselves. It helps our peace of mind if we can accept that we are just teaching children the best habits we can. We hope that they remember our instructions and latch onto the habits more when they leave home.

Whether you're dealing with an adult or a child, you may be in a situation where you simply have to correct the problem yourself and move forward. The best thing you can do is accept what is occurring, get the project done as quickly as possible, and focus heavily on preventing it from happening in the future.

Motivational Barrier #7: *Hopelessness*

Does your situation feel futile, like no matter what you do, it will just get this way again? If you have a recurring problem area in your home, it helps to step back from it, give it some serious consideration, and think through the problem from the very root.

- Where is this problem originating?

- Is there a pattern here?

- What is the "chain of custody" of these items—where did they come from?

- Can I stop the inflow of items in some way?

If you have access to an objective person who can help you think through this, it can make all the difference. You may be too close to the problem to see what is going on. A friend or Professional Organizer can help, and if you're a member of our program you can certainly ask us in our message boards.

Along with thinking through your process, remember that maintenance is part of that process too—that is why this book has a whole section on it! We have to brush our teeth every day, for example. It's a fact of life, and so are many other things, especially when it comes to home ownership. Decide for yourself how disorganized an area can get before it becomes uncomfortable to you, and accept the fact that it must be maintained by someone.

Consider lowering your standards if that makes you feel happier and less stressed in your home. When I became a mother I figured out pretty quickly that I had to lower my standards of "cleanliness" if I was going to stay sane! A certain amount of toys and things will always remain out, and you may not have time to clean the house as often as you would like. It takes some mental adjustments and time to get to a level of acceptance about having different standards, but it can be done.

If you feel hopeless because you have struggled with disorganization your entire life, and your home feels overwhelming, you might read more about "chronic disorganization." The National Study Group on Chronic Disorganization website at www.nsgcd.org has many resources for you. Organizing challenges often stem from "situational" issues and major transitions such as moving, having children and changing jobs. But if you feel these issues are much more pervasive and lasting, you might need to get additional assistance beyond reading this book. I highly encourage you to read about the "Clutter Hoarding Scale" and look at the "Fact Sheets" they have on this website.

Motivational Barrier #8: *Perfectionism*

Ironically, perfectionism can be the root cause of procrastination, resulting in some very large organizing challenges. The reason is that it's a form of "All or Nothing Thinking." In other words, "If I can't do it perfectly, I don't want to do it at all." Perfectionism can also be related to a fear of failure and a strong need for approval. Do you relate to this?

As you might guess, many people in my profession talk about being "Recovering Perfectionists," and I am one also. I keep a little reminder card in my office that shows a man clipping blades of grass with nail scissors, and it says, "Did you remember to forget perfection?" I now strive for doing *excellent* work but not *perfect* work. One of the best things I have learned to say is, "Oh, well! It just doesn't matter." And then LET IT GO.

Perfection is an unattainable goal. It doesn't exist! There IS such a thing as "Good Enough," and I really believe that is one of the most important concepts in this book. What is logically better—doing nothing, or doing something? Sometimes just realizing you're playing this mental game with yourself is enough to push you forward.

The best step to take if you are grappling with perfectionism is to get unstuck. Get advice or missing information if you need it, and give yourself a deadline with some accountability to another person. In some cases, talking with a counseling professional can be very helpful if your perfectionism is affecting your relationships and your career.

Motivational Barrier #9: *Time and Energy Deficit*

Do you find yourself saying, "I am just too tired and I don't have time to get organized"? A survey done by Day Runner found that 65% of people described themselves as "very" or "insanely" busy. *Psychology Today* found that more than 90% of those in their survey declare an overwhelming sense of "time-poverty," part of an epidemic of anxiety and pressure in our society.

I have found in many cases there actually is time, but people are making choices that make that time evaporate. There are many people out there, especially women, who are *simply doing too much.*

First look at your time in general. What things can you get off your plate? If you read the popular book *I Don't Know How She Does It: The Life of Kate Reddy, Working Mother* by Allison Pearson, you may remember the opening scene when she is "distressing" pies from the grocery store at one in the morning to make them look homemade to send to school. Sometimes we create standards for ourselves that are unrealistic. You do NOT have to make everything from scratch, volunteer for everything, and do everything yourself. It's really okay to ask for help and take some shortcuts! (See our previous information on how to cross things off your list in Chapter 1.)

Make sure you're taking care of yourself. I have heard experts on life balance remind us that when the oxygen masks drop from the ceiling of the airplane, the instructions are to put your mask on first before assisting other passengers. Of course! You can't help anybody if you are passed out! My friend Renee Trudeau has a helpful book called *The Mother's Guide to Self-Renewal: How to Reclaim, Rejuvenate and Re-Balance Your Life.* She even has a growing community of "Personal Renewal Groups" that have sprung up around the country to support one another in these efforts.

Some of our clients have been wise enough to actually take vacation days to organize. What is better: going to the beach and coming home to the same mess, in debt with a giant stack of mail to go through, or... spending a few days at home getting it to the condition that supports you to continue your life and work in a renewed and energized way?

Remember that procrastinated projects actually rob you of your energy. Spiritual teacher John-Roger says, "If you leave incomplete projects to abound, they 'sting' the unconscious and drag on you. You may be unaware of the cause, but the effect will be your walking around feeling heavy, with the low-energy blues. Even after you sleep like the dead for ten hours, you'll still think you need a great deal of sleep. It's called the karma of incompletions."

We have a free report available to our readers called *30 Ways to Find Time to Get Organized.* When you sign up for our weekly e-mail newsletter, we'll send you a link to the report, and if you're a member of our site, the report is available in our Knowledge Base.

Motivational Barrier #10: *Boredom*

Does the thought of doing your organizing projects and the maintenance tasks in your home just feel incredibly, mind-numbingly boring? It is a reality that everyone has tasks to do that they don't enjoy. The very first line of one of the most popular self-help books of all time, *The Road Less Traveled*

by M. Scott Peck, states simply, "Life is difficult." Happiness comes in the true acceptance of this fact. This basic truth means we have to get creative and find ways to push ourselves through the difficulty.

In our next chapter, we will be discussing ways of making things interesting and fun. These suggestions hold the cure for the boredom problem!

Clutter Fitness Exercises

- Write down the defeatist language you've used in the past and RE-write it in a way that supports you to make changes.

- What are the two barriers you most identify with in your situation? How could you push through them? If you need help, paid members can log into our site and get advice from our team.

- It's time to think about your own support system. Who can you be accountable to for your goals? How would you like to set this up for yourself? List three people who might be Motivation Partners with you and a way that you might best work with each of them.

How to Overcome Inertia

Because the root of all disorganization is delayed decisions and actions, procrastination is really the cause of almost all clutter in your home and your life. We have seen it time and time again that the biggest obstacle to making progress is simply getting started. It can be the hardest thing to do, and that is because it's actually a law of nature that makes that so!

In science class you may have heard of Newton's First Law of Motion:

> An object at rest tends to stay at rest and an object in motion tends to stay in motion with the same speed and in the same direction unless acted upon by an unbalanced force.

These tendencies of staying either at rest or in motion are called INERTIA. What does this mean in plain English?

A soccer ball "in motion," whether flying through the air or rolling on the ground, will stay in motion unless it's acted upon by the "unbalanced force" of gravity that causes it to fall to the ground and eventually roll to a stop. That same soccer ball, once it's stopped or "at rest," will remain at rest until another "unbalanced force" like a kick sets it in motion again.

> Inertia has two sides to it: The positive effect of having the tendency of remaining in motion, causing progress and action; and the negative effect of having the tendency to remain at rest, causing inactivity and stagnation.

Inertia examples from our lives:

- **The Couch Potato:** Inertia at rest. The Couch Potato needs an unbalanced force of hunger or something else to get up and get moving.

- **Pushing the Snooze Button:** Inertia at rest. We need an unbalanced force of the fear of being late, or at least "the call of nature," to get up and get moving.

- **"Getting On a Roll":** Have you ever intended to just pull a few weeds and then found yourself weeding the entire yard? Or have you ever intended to read only one chapter of a book and ended up not being able to put it down? Some people call this experience being "in a flow state" or "in the zone." Those are great examples of inertia "in motion."

> **One of the biggest secrets of this book:**
> Once you can overcome "at rest" inertia to get started, this same tendency can make you keep going! It's actually a law of nature!

Your determination, your will, is often the unbalanced force required to overcome "at rest" inertia. Sometimes, however, like when faced with a big piece of chocolate, will is not quite enough! Thankfully there are many helpful methods of giving yourself a "kick." In the last chapter, if you identified with "Boredom" as a Motivational Barrier, you'll be able to use these ideas to help make your organizing more fun and interesting.

Six ways to kick yourself in the pants to get started

One way to get started is to "Tell the World." Or at least just tell a friend! We have a "Public Declarations" forum in the private member area of our site where people declare their intentions and come back to report what happened. One of our members even started her own separate public blog about what she is doing. That tactic is not for everyone, but posting "before" photos is incredibly motivating! Again, there is nothing like being accountable to another human being to make you push through that inertia of getting started.

You can also use a timer to make a little game of getting started. Promise yourself you only have to work on something for a defined period of time like 15 minutes or one hour, and give yourself permission to stop completely when that time is over. If you want to work continuously, you can try working for 45 minutes and taking a break for 15 minutes. You'll often find that "in motion" inertia takes over and you really want to keep going!

Take a moment to find the kind of timer that works best for you. Some people like the old-fashioned kind that audibly ticks as it goes, because it's like a constant reminder, redirecting your attention back to the project. You might also want to get one that goes in your pocket or clips onto your belt and has a vibrate setting, in case you like listening to music while you work and can't hear a normal timer. Or, just use the "sleep timer" on an iPod so that the music stops when you want to stop (found in the "Clock" menu).

Thinking about your goal as a huge overwhelming mountain to climb makes **it even more difficult to overcome inertia and get started.** It's helpful to break up your big goals into smaller, manageable bites that are more easily achievable. For example, I am writing this book one chapter at a time. If I think about writing "The Whole Book" it can feel ominous!

Our members use our weekly project plans to help them break down their goals. They also describe their projects to our experts. We help them make a plan and give them incremental "homework" assignments to get it done.

The enticement of a reward is a huge motivator for getting started! Think about what animal researchers have known for a long time: You can train an animal to do almost anything if they get a reward for doing it. If you want the mouse to push the button, give him a piece of cheese every time he does it. We are really no different! *Anything we do repeatedly by choice has some kind of intrinsic reward.* In fact, researchers say it is absolutely CRUCIAL to reward yourself when you are making progress. It reinforces your sense of success on a much deeper level and allows you to feel acknowledged and appreciated.

The weekly plans on our website have a "dessert" which is a suggested reward each week for doing your projects. For example, if we are doing our quick "BBCA" project, which is culling through your Bulletin Boards, Coupons & Artwork, we might suggest the dessert of using a special coupon or gift certificate that week that you've found in the process.

What carrot could you dangle in front of yourself to get something big done? Our members and clients have been known to get massages, go out for a special dinner, buy an exceptional bottle of wine, or watch their favorite guilty pleasure TV show at the end of the day. Whatever is important and fun to you is what will work.

Make it interesting! If you are so inclined, make a bet with someone. A wager, after all, is just a twist on having a reward—with a bit of competition and accountability built in. You can have a contest with a friend based on which one of you finishes a project first, or set a deadline to see if each of you can meet it.

Make it fun and enjoyable. One of the best ways to add enjoyment is listening to audiobooks while you work on your projects. I am always using my iPod with audiobooks that I have downloaded to make the time melt away when I am working on housework or organizing projects. "Hey, wow! Who just organized the refrigerator? Oh, wait, that was me." I literally lose track of time because I am so engrossed in my book. You can get audiobooks at the library, at used bookstores, and online from Audible.com.

Your favorite music can also add fun to the equation, and music is preferable to audiobooks when you are doing projects that require more mental focus. Managing paper and filing or anything else that requires you to make serious decisions and go through mental processes will be less effective if your brain is also trying to process the plot of your audiobook. You will be spreading your brainpower too thin! You may even need to choose music with minimal lyrics if you find it too distracting. But music can definitely pace you, pep you up, and make you smile! Try it.

Working with a friend is probably the number one way to make projects fun. The other benefits of this method are tremendous, such as getting your friend's objective opinion on your "stuff" and his or her ideas on your puzzling storage problems. Be careful not to talk so much that it's distracting from the project at hand and slowing you down. But your friend's help can reduce the time required, distract you from the boredom, and give you some great laughs and memories.

Clutter Fitness Exercises

- Write in your workbook what kind of "unbalanced force" you could apply to yourself that would bust through YOUR inertia.

- How can you make your organizing projects more fun and interesting? List two ideas from this chapter that you could apply right away.

- Contact one of the people you listed in the last chapter's exercises as a possible Motivation Partner and explain what you'd like to do. It's time to start getting a commitment from one of them to work on each others' goals. Remember, your goals do not have the same!

Prevention

Don't Let Clutter in the Door

Have you ever heard the dieting proverb, "A moment on the lips, a lifetime on the hips"? Obviously it takes eating the donuts to make them show up somewhere on your body later!

When you're trying to lose weight, you've got to stop eating the donuts...preventing additional weight gain where it begins. It's no different for your home! Preventing clutter from getting in the door is one of the best strategies for reducing your clutter immediately and over time.

Get Your Greens

In terms of building a healthy body, everyone has probably heard the sage advice to "get your greens." Eating salads and dark leafy greens adds a powerhouse of nutrition to your diet and replaces less healthful junk food. So when you're building a healthy home and planet, we want you to "get your greens" by considering greener, more environmentally-sensitive choices. We'll be adding our *Get Your Greens* thoughts and tips throughout the book.

Consuming less overall is obviously a "green" idea and aspiration. Did you know that...

- "Most Europeans produce less than half the waste per person as the average American." [4]
- "The average American home grew from 983 square feet in 1950 to 2,434 square feet in 2005." That increase is more than DOUBLE. [5]
- "The size of the average American family has shrunk over the last three decades... Today's average family size is 2.6 people. [In 1974], it was 3.1 people." [6]

As Americans, we have much smaller families than before and double the amount of space for ourselves! We produce twice as much waste as Europeans, and we have an endless supply of "MORE."

To lose Clutter-Pounds[SM], we need to stop or reduce the amount of unneeded things from coming into the house—*right now.* Not only do we get the benefit of less volume of clutter, but we can save money too!

Where does clutter come from?

Clutter enters your life in these 3 ways:

1. **Purchasing:** you are paying money to bring it into your home

2. **Acquiring:** you are receiving the clutter from someone or somewhere else

3. **Allowing:** permitting non-physical clutter to occupy your time and energy, such as time commitments and communication clutter

The next 3 chapters will focus on each of these and how specifically to reduce them.

High-Calorie Clutter

Here are some common, easily preventable purchasing and acquiring decisions that are not needed or missed and are highly impactful on the home in terms of wasted space and excess bulk. Watch out for too much of these!

- Arts and crafts supplies
- Books
- Collectibles, such as dishes or figurines
- Excess shoes and clothing
- Jewelry and wardrobe accessories
- Garage sale/flea market finds
- Magazines and Newspapers
- Media—DVDs, VHS, and CDs
- School and work papers
- Toys

Clutter Fitness Exercise

Which way is clutter entering your life more: Purchasing, Acquiring, or Allowing?

In my youth
I stressed freedom,
and in my old age
I stress order. I have
made the great
discovery that liberty
is a product of order.

–Will Durant

Purchasing Clutter

Purchased clutter is the easiest kind to prevent, because you have full control! You actually have to pay money to bring these items into your home, and saving money by *not* buying more things can be a big motivating factor.

Think before you buy

There are 5 important Clutter Prevention questions to ask before you buy something:

Who owns this already and might share it with me?
What do I already have that is like this?
Where will this be stored?
When will I have time to use it and maintain it?
Why do I want to buy this?

We have created a free printable "wallet reminder sleeve" with these questions on it, to prevent clutter where it starts! You can store your credit or debit cards in these sleeves so that you are reminded of what to ask when you are in the actual purchasing process. You can get information about downloading these at www.clutterdiet.com/book. You will also find a video there that shows how they work.

Using these Clutter Prevention questions is like having an organizing expert on your shoulder! I remember shopping with a client once who, along with the organizing supplies we needed, wanted to buy a large "Fry Daddy" electric frying vat. She had a recipe in mind that she wanted to try, and having this fryer was going to make it easier. I asked her one of the most important Clutter Prevention questions, "Where will this be stored?" It stopped her in her tracks! She realized this large specialty appliance would not easily find a home in her kitchen cabinets, and further realized that this was something she would seldom use. Furthermore, it would take time to learn how to use and clean the fryer. She decided to use her large cast iron skillet instead, thereby saving herself time, money, and space all at once!

Plan before you shop

Do you remember the Yellow Pages advertisements that used to say "Let your fingers do the walking"? The idea was that you can use the phone to call ahead and get information on pricing and availability before leaving home. Now we would most likely do much of this legwork online, but researching your purchases is smarter than ever given the volume of options we have. Some great online shopping comparison tools are:

- www.pricegrabber.com
- www.nextag.com
- www.mysimon.com
- http://shopping.yahoo.com
- www.roboshopper.com
- www.dealtime.com
- www.pricerunner.com
- www.shopping.com

Have all the information you need before you leave home to shop. Consider the wasted time involved in returning unneeded items to the store! Many of our clients also have a considerable amount of clutter that consists of items that should have been returned but they waited too long to do it. Take measurements and write them down. Bring color swatches, pictures, or samples that are needed to make a decision, particularly for decorative items where color is important.

You may want to make a "shopping notebook" if you have a lot of home decorating or other purchasing to do all at once. Get a small, unused photo album or 3-ring binder that is easy to carry along, and use it to hold your paint swatches, fabric samples, and other items. You can even have a page for each room with photos of the space and its furniture, with measurements for each item if needed.

Keep a grocery shopping list so you'll know what you need, and teach your family to write down things they use up and want to replace. This simple practice reduces trips to the store and also creates fewer impulse purchases. Did you know that between 51 and 68 percent of grocery store purchases are impulse buys?[7] The stores are counting on this fact! They stack the ends of the aisles ("endcaps") and the checkout lanes with tempting extras that are probably not on your list but seem like good ideas at the time.

Combine your grocery shopping list with meal planning, and you've got one of the best ways to prevent purchased clutter and wasted money. Spending ten to fifteen minutes to write up a quick plan for a week of dinners and a corresponding shopping list can save you hours of time and reduce the six o'clock stress of "what's for dinner." (We'll cover this more thoroughly in Chapter 18, Creating Your Meals System.)

Review your closet before shopping for new clothes. If you've organized your closet well (which we will be covering in our *Room by Room Recipes* section), you'll have full visibility to your wardrobe. If you can easily see that you own three pink track suits, it's unlikely you'll buy another one. You can keep a notepad in your closet for making notes on things that need repairing or replacing, or things you notice you might need to buy (like a scarf to go with a certain blouse).

Quick, you need to buy some shower sandals for summer camp… is your son's shoe size a 9 or a 10? Knowing the sizes of your family and other significant people is a great time-saver if you are buying clothing for them. You can easily keep this information in your PDA or your day planner, or even on a piece of paper in your wallet. You may want to write the information down in pencil, though, if your kids grow as fast as mine do!

Practice "Portion Control"

In the weight loss world, one of the best tricks to lose weight is to pay attention to portion control. Is a serving really half a cup, but you're eating a whole cup? You can cut your calorie intake drastically by paying attention to portions. Clutter calories are no different! If you come home from the store with less, you have less clutter to deal with later. Remember when shopping that people make their life's work figuring out how to sell to you, and they are very clever. Here are some of the purchasing traps that make you buy more than you intended:

- **The "one in every color" trap.** If you like this in white, wouldn't you also love to have it in brown? You might as well get it while you're here, right? Think carefully and make sure you are not being impulsive.

- **The "collect them all!" trap.** Kids are particularly vulnerable to this ploy, with action figures and trading cards. But many adults are also prone to "collectibles" like figurines and ornaments. Make sure they are something you'll really enjoy and use and that you're not just buying something for the sake of having the whole set. Certainly there are times when a complete set of something is more valuable than a few pieces, like fine china. But asking the Clutter Prevention questions at the beginning of this chapter should help.

- **The "free gift with purchase" trap.** We see this trap most often from cosmetics counters. Many of the free bonus makeup items are in odd colors that never get used, and the small skin care items are often forgotten in a drawer. If you are buying it primarily for the fabulous zippered bag, consider if your money would be better spent just buying a similar bag instead! Or do you even need that? We have seen clients with a pile of those free gift bags that go unused. Remember that the free gift is often tied to a minimum purchase price too, which means you may buy more than you planned to get yourself above the minimum.

- **The "bigger is better" trap.** Warehouse clubs bundle six cans of pineapple slices with plastic shrink wrap, so if you just needed one can you are now buying all six, and you are rationalizing that they won't go bad. Just because it's packaged that way doesn't mean it's a good idea, particularly if you have a small family. Buy bigger bundles only if you have room to store the items and if they are not perishable.

- **The "free shipping" trap.** You learn that if you buy only a few more dollars' worth of purchases online you are eligible for free shipping, and you quickly start searching around for something else to buy. Is this really valid logic? Only if you think of something else you truly needed and intended to buy.

- **The "it's on sale" trap.** Remember that even if something's on sale, if you shouldn't buy it in the first place, it doesn't matter.

Control your "clutter cravings."

People often seem to have an appetite for purchasing certain things, but just like food cravings, you really can overcome your urge to collect. Here are some examples of places that can be the clutter calorie equivalent of going to Krispy Kreme:

- Garage sales
- Flea markets
- Souvenir shops
- Discount stores
- Used bookstores
- Shoe stores

Get comfortable with the concept of "enough." Avoid the places that encourage your particular collecting behavior, and if you must go, have a targeted approach to something you've planned ahead to buy. You may even need to bring a friend to "talk you down."

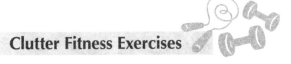

Clutter Fitness Exercises

- What are two ideas from this chapter that you can implement right away?
- Get our free Clutter Prevention Wallet Reminder Sleeves when you sign up for our newsletter at www.clutterdiet.com/book. Cut and fold them and put them in your wallet to remind you of all you learned in this chapter.

Like so many Americans, she was trying to construct a life that made sense from things she found in gift shops.

\- Kurt Vonnegut, Slaughterhouse Five

Acquiring Clutter

Sometimes "clutter happens." Let's explore the six origins of the clutter that you don't pay for, or even really ask for. Where does it come from, and how do you stop it?

Acquired Clutter Source #1: *Your Mailbox*

Every day (except for Sundays) the mail carrier brings even more paper to you. Some of our clients have been so overwhelmed that they just stashed the mail in paper bags and put them in the closet, putting off the inevitable.

According to NewDream.org and the U.S. Postal Service, more than 300 pieces of bulk mail are sent out per year for every man, woman, and child! (In my experience, that actually sounds low.) And the Consumer Research Institute says that Americans throw away 44% of bulk mail unopened, yet still spend eight months per lifetime opening bulk mail.

There are two keys to solving the junk mail problem: processing and prevention.

Mail Processing: Process your mail as you would your dishes. *What is your tolerance for leaving dishes in the sink?* Can you stand to leave them overnight, a couple of days, or not at all? I find from audiences' responses that most people typically do not want to leave dishes more than a day or so. Whatever your personal tolerance for stacking up dishes, there is a reason for that short period of time. You know that the dishes are going to keep coming! The continuous flow means that you must process them. Now, transfer that thinking to your mail... your mail is also going to keep coming, like a mighty, unstoppable river. If you don't process it and let it flow back out, it's going to dam up and drown you!

Have one designated place where the mail sits ready to be processed. Think of it as "To Be Sorted." You can use a basket or tray and keep it near the door where you enter and exit the house. As your kitchen sink is to dishes, your sorting basket is to mail! Keep a large trashcan nearby, along with a couple of quality letter openers. When the mail comes in, plop it right into this basket.

As you reach your "dishes tolerance" on it, no more than two days, sort the mail. Here are the categories for quick sorting, the "ART" of managing paper (more on "ART" and paper management later):

- **Action:** Anything that requires your action, such as bills, forms, or items that require a phone call. A special Action subcategory is reading material. Pull this out first. You may find that the bulk of your mail pile reduces tremendously getting this out of the way, and the remainder probably will feel less intimidating.

- **Reference:** Anything you simply need to keep but does not require any action on your part. These Reference items are things you will want to file in your filing system, so we recommend a "To Be Filed" basket in your home office area.

- **Trash:** Hopefully you have a lot of this category. This means junk mail! Don't forget to shred mail that is potentially damaging to your finances, privacy, or reputation.

Get Your Greens

Try to recycle whatever you can in this process! Many recycling programs accept "anything that tears," which means most junk mail and catalogs will be taken. Check with your local disposal service to learn about specifics for your neighborhood.

Mail Prevention: Don't make it easy for them. If you order from catalogs, subscribe to magazines, send in warranty registration cards, or enter sweepstakes or other contests, you will probably be placed on a mailing list. If you do these things, you need to specify that you do not want to receive solicitations or have your contact information shared or sold. Contests are often designed specifically to get contact information, and warranty cards are often unnecessary to send. Reconsider spending your time doing these tasks.

Take your name off the lists when you can. For residential mail, ask to have your name registered with the Mail Preference Service. You will need to do this every three years, and it covers only nationally distributed mail—not local mail. You can do this online at www.dmachoice.org.

Get off the lists of the major credit reporting agencies. There is one easy, 24-hour number to call to accomplish this, or you can go to www.optoutprescreen.com. The phone number is 1-888-567-8688. When you call this number you will be directed to specify your contact information, including your Social Security number. This service already has your Social Security number, so it is a legitimate request to verify your identity. Follow the instructions to have your name removed permanently. You can also stay on the line and repeat the process for a spouse or other family member at your address. This is one of the best and easiest things you can do—it takes less than five minutes.

There are services that do some of this work for you. A website called 41pounds.org, so named because the average adult receives forty-one pounds of junk mail per year, claims to reduce your junk mail by 80-95%! It costs $41 for five years of coverage, and they donate a significant portion to nonprofit groups. Some of our members like ProQuo.com, a free service that is similar.

Take preventative measures when catalog shopping. Specifically ask to be excluded from solicitations and mailings when you place your order by phone. If you shop online, check the website's privacy policy and make sure checkboxes for receiving communications remain unchecked before pressing the "go" button on your order. If you are already on their mailing lists, it's simple to call the company's toll free number or send an e-mail to remove your name. You can also utilize a free service just for catalogs called CatalogChoice.org—a great resource!

Having your own form letter makes quick work of unsubscribing. Send a form out easily when you want to be removed from a mailer's list. Members of our site can access our printable 4"x6" postcard template in Microsoft Word format, found in our Knowledge Base, or you can make your own with something similar to the message below.

To Whom It May Concern:

Please do not share, sell, rent, or in any other way give my contact information to any other party for purposes of e-mail, phone, or paper mail communication. Please exclude me from any mailings, paper or electronic, and any phone solicitations originating from your company as well.

Thank you,

(your name)
(your address)
(your phone number- if appropriate)

Acquired Clutter Source #2: *Gifts*

In anthropology studies, "reciprocity" is a fascinating aspect to study about human cultures. Who is giving what to whom and when? Some cultures give frequent gifts for many social reasons, with lots of ritual surrounding them, and expectations are high for not only the gift itself but also for the adherence to these rituals. Japan is famous for its particular gift-giving etiquette, including the custom of always presenting a gift with two hands.

What is the anthropology of gift-giving in your family and social circle? We must graciously accept gifts for social propriety, but we sometimes end up with clutter as a result. What can we do about this "special" clutter coming into our lives?

Start at the source—ask for what you want! Many gift-givers who are close to you would be grateful for information about items you actually would enjoy and use. Sometimes I see something when I am out with my mother and wink at her and say, "That would make a great holiday gift for me." She appreciates it and makes a mental note. My family asks for wish lists from one another during holiday and birthday times. Your family may think this is horrible, but at least be proactive and keep a list of what you

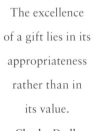

The excellence of a gift lies in its appropriateness rather than in its value.
- Charles Dudley Warner

want for when someone asks! And dropping hints is almost never a bad idea… you can tell one person who can indirectly let another person know your wishes. It's all in good fun! The goals for everyone should be to enjoy the process, give things people will actually love and use, and delight in the pleasure of giving.

If your family is open to discussing issues like these, try having a conversation about simplifying the gift-giving overall, especially during the winter holidays. Broaching this subject often reveals tremendous relief for all involved! Here are some approaches you could propose and discuss:

- **Drawing names:** Put all adult family members' names in a drawing to determine for each person who will be the recipient of one special gift. When you receive the name of your recipient, you can keep it a secret if you think that is more fun, or you can have an open conversation about whom you are gifting. You might want to have a spending range or limit so things feel fair all around. Focusing on just one person saves a tremendous amount of shopping time and allows you to make that gift a special and meaningful one.

- **Spending limits:** You might decide that you each still want to give gifts to everyone, but you could agree that nobody spends more than a certain amount, such as $25.

- **Kids only:** If your family includes numerous siblings with many of their own children, you can all buy only for the kids and not worry about the adults.

- **Pitching in for one larger gift for someone special:** You might agree that all siblings pitch in for a large gift to the parents instead of buying for each other. My husband and his siblings once bought a new dining table and chairs for their parents.

- **No gifts at all:** You may decide that you'll all take a trip somewhere together (a cruise is perfect for this) and forego all gifts. Or, you could all work together on a charity project instead of giving gifts.

- **Small or homemade gifts only:** Another approach is to give small gifts only, like stocking stuffers at Christmas. I know some families who mandate homemade gifts only, so that the gifts are unique and personal (and typically edible!).

Set an example with your own "Low Clutter-Calorie" gift-giving practices. Beyond your immediate family, there are still ways to reduce the impact of gift clutter. If appropriate, explain to those you are gifting that you feel we are all abundantly blessed with possessions and that you would rather celebrate your relationship by purchasing something more practical and meaningful. Here are some ideas for "Low Clutter-Calorie" gifting:

- Gift certificates to a store they frequent (iTunes gift cards are great for iPod lovers!)
- Classes you could take together, like continuing education, art or cooking classes
- Experiences, like a trip to the zoo or an aquarium
- Memberships to museums or to a website like Clutter Diet
- Edible gifts or a meal at a special restaurant
- Donations made in their name to a worthy cause

Anything that has real and lasting value is always a gift from within.

-Franz Kafka

So what do you do when you receive gifts that you don't want or need? Please give yourself permission to return them or otherwise let them go. If you think that someone will notice when visiting that you're not using it, keep in mind they probably won't, unless it's a painting they intended for you to keep over the mantle (in which case you really just need to have a frank conversation!). If you're keeping items like this, you may be harboring some unrealistic fears about what the person would think. You have to do what is right for you, and continuing to store something you do not love and never use is a waste and a disservice to yourself. Let that item find a good home where someone else will appreciate it.

Acquired Clutter Source #3: *School & Work*

Every time you return home and walk in the door, you are potentially bringing in new clutter. The first step to reducing this is to be mindful of this fact! Your children may bring in papers from school, and you may have samples, equipment, paperwork, and reading material from work.

Consider whether you really need to bring things home from work, and strive for a separation of your work life and home life if possible. Are the things you're bringing home going to go right back out with you when you leave again, or are they quietly just getting stored in your house? Are you kidding yourself that you're going to read those professional journals during your leisure time? Maybe someday in an alternate universe? If you are storing enough work-related items that it's interfering with your space, you can question whether your employer should really take responsibility for some of that.

If you are self-employed, you may have more difficult questions in this regard. Try to confine the work-related materials to one or two rooms or storage areas, and if you don't have outside office space, revisit the question periodically of whether you really should. Many of our entrepreneur clients who started businesses from home have been tremendously happier since they made the decision to sign a lease for office space and get the work-related clutter out of their houses.

Your children's school papers need to be dealt with frequently, either daily or weekly as the situation requires. You'll be able to sort through them the same way you sort through your mail using the "ART" acronym from earlier in this chapter. Keep important reference papers in a family binder, such as policies and schedules. If there are uncertain, potential reference items, as there will be, we recommend a "Limiting Container" that provides a cue for you to cull through the papers. A rectangular basket or tray, not too deep, is a great limiting container with the idea that you must clean out the tray when it gets full. Members can read much more about children's artwork and papers in the Knowledge Base on our website.

Acquired Clutter Source #4: *Freebies*

Hold on a minute with those hand-me-downs! You may receive offers of clothing, books, furniture, and other items that your family and friends no longer need. If you really will use and enjoy these items, that is terrific. Some people genuinely benefit from exchanging things like maternity or children's clothing. But if you're accepting things to be polite, beware… and remember, *"A moment on the lips, a lifetime on the hips!"* As soon as those items cross the threshold into your home, they are potentially going to remain there as clutter. Either graciously refuse the items, or donate them yourself right away and move them out.

"But they were just giving them away!" You've just had a great week at your industry's trade show, and you're packing to come home. STOP! Don't bring home those freebies you are never going to use. Better yet, don't pick them up on the convention floor in the first place. Nobody really needs another Frisbee, calculator, or t-shirt. We recommend going through all of the goody-bags and session handouts before packing them and allowing them to cross the threshold of the house. This includes the little hotel soaps and shampoos, unless you really do use them at home! Just because they are "perfectly useful" does not mean they are necessarily useful for YOU.

Acquired Clutter Source #5: *Inheritance*

The death of a parent or other close relative often means you bewilderingly and suddenly find yourself dealing with a large number of someone else's personal possessions. The unique challenge with this kind of acquired clutter is that the items almost all *feel* sentimental but really are not that special to you. Your grief and your memories mean that everything you see reminds you of that person you've lost, and it's "her" tissue paper holder and "her" candles and "her" handwritten grocery list. Your emotions can make it much more difficult to make decisions.

If you can, try to decide upon these items in an outside location away from your own home, and avoid bringing them into your own home before decisions are made. When possible, have an objective third party assist you with making decisions on these possessions.

We once had a client who inherited a prolific writer's estate, including the rights to his work, which would be referenced and built upon probably forever. The client was a distant relative but was the only heir, and suddenly and unexpectedly their home was overtaken by boxes and boxes of papers, extra copies of books and magazines, and even prototypes of proposed toys and other merchandise related to the books' characters. They inherited a lifetime of managing this deceased person's creative output and needed to field inquiries immediately about reprints and rights. Fascinating! They definitely needed to hire someone to assist them. Your inheritance is probably not this complex, but the need for outside help when you are suddenly faced with perplexing decisions is crucial. Please don't try to do everything yourself! If you inherited money as part of the estate, it's worth it to use some of that money to get the help you need. You may be able to choose a few items you want and have an estate liquidator help you handle the rest of the items.

Overall, remember that you can't possibly keep it all. You'll need to prioritize what the most important memories of that person are and keep a few items that will memorialize them appropriately. Remember that the objects are just objects, that nothing will take the place of that actual person, and that you will still hold all of the memories of the item in your head even if the actual item is not in your house. There are other ways of memorializing your loved one's things, such as taking a photo of yourself with certain objects before selling or donating them.

Acquired Clutter Source #6: *Children/Family Storage*

When children leave home for college, they leave behind many of their possessions and the furniture they were using. Then, when they finish college and leave home for good, they still may abandon some of those belongings for you to store. After they get their first jobs and their own homes, it's no longer appropriate for you to store these items for your adult children. At some point, you need to say "claim it or lose it!" We've had clients storing an entire garage bay full of items for their adult children. You need to free up this space for the activities that mean something to your own life right now. Maybe you could have a new office, exercise, or craft room if only you were not storing your children's things!

We've been assuming in the above paragraph that your children want you to store these items for them, but what if the opposite is true? Are you storing things like furniture, toys, and appliances because you think your children surely will want these "perfectly good" items? *Do they really?* We once had a client who was keeping three storage units full of "stuff" for her children who, in reality, did not want the items at all. They had homes and lives and children of their own, and they had their own furniture in other cities and states. If you have asked your children more than once and they have not expressed interest or claimed the items, chances are they really don't want them.

E-mail is a great medium for distributing items in your family that you no longer want to store. You can take photos of the items in question and attach them to an e-mail message to your children. Include a list of everything along with important details, the most important of which is the deadline you're going to give them to claim the items and arrange for their shipment. Once this date is past, you'll find another home for these items by selling them or donating them. Make sure they understand you are firm! And if it's really impossible for them to claim the items due to an understandable delay, a compromise might be that you move them to a storage unit in their name and have the bill sent to them. Life is short—don't wait on someone else to allow you to create that new exercise room or park that car in the garage. Use your own home the way YOU want to!

Clutter Fitness Exercises

- Take action for 15 minutes on some of the junk mail reducing strategies in this chapter.
- What actions could you take to reduce Acquired Clutter in these areas?
    - Mailbox
    - Gifts
    - Work
    - Freebies
    - Inheritance
    - Children/Family Storage

Allowing Clutter

We've looked at the physical clutter that comes right into the door, but there are also two kinds of "invisible clutter" you are allowing into your life without even realizing it!

Time Clutter

Excessive time commitments are the primary type of invisible clutter. In the same way that a house or a closet has only a limited amount of space, your calendar has only a limited amount of time. Your calendar can be just as cluttered as your basement, and it may be worse because you feel the effects more on a daily basis.

Are you a "pleaser?" Oprah Winfrey writes a column for the last page of her magazine called, "What I Know For Sure." I kept one of the columns in which she wrote about realizing that she has the right to change her mind, and that you have the right to choose what is best for you *now*. She says, "...[A]s strict as I had always been about keeping my word, I often gave it irresponsibly. Trying to be the nice girl, I agreed to do things I later regretted. And because I was saying yes when I really meant no, I'd end up cheating both myself and the other person involved."

Do you resent certain appointments on your calendar? Have you found your mouth uttering the word "Yes," or found your hand rising up in the air to volunteer, at the same time your mind is screaming "Don't do it"? How does that happen? Is the word "should" involved?

Are you an "overdoer?" I am often amazed at the list of activities we hear about our clients and members doing. Each of these activities taken alone is a valid and admirable pursuit, but in combination they are a recipe for overload, stress, and even illness. Add up more than three or four of them and you will need to be fitted for a superhero cape. How many of these are *you* doing?

- Parenting
- Working outside the home
- Running a side business (or two)
- Caring for aging parents
- Caring for pets
- Homeschooling
- Volunteering at church or temple
- Volunteering at school
- Volunteering for charities
- Volunteering for leadership in kids' activities (coach's helper, scout leader)
- Cooking everything from scratch
- Growing and canning food
- Making your own clothing and costumes

> We need to find the courage to say NO to the things and people that are not serving us if we want to rediscover ourselves and live our lives with authenticity.
>
> - **Barbara DeAngelis**

- Hosting too many social and family events
- Driving around to multiple stores to save a few cents per item
- Extensively documenting your family's lives with video and photos and creating elaborate scrapbooks

Let's think back to the days of the American pioneers. A good portion of a woman's day was spent making sure there was a fire in the hearth so that she could cook and keep her family warm, and we can achieve the same at the flip of a switch. Food was not only cooked from scratch, but often the food had to be gathered or hunted for hours. Dishwashers, indoor plumbing, washing machines, cars, grocery stores, and telephones were not a part of their lives. These women's entire days were spent providing the most basic of needs.

Now that we have those basic needs systematized and we have time for higher level pursuits, we somehow feel like we are supposed to pack in as much other activity as possible. Do we have a washing machine and dryer so we can have more "leisure" time, or do we take that time and apply it to the Girl Scout Community Garage Sale? Are we so busy that we don't have time to enjoy the fruits of our labors?

Martha Stewart and the extension of her personal brand into magazines, paint, linens, furniture, and even entire homes, has definitely given the world a bit more grace and elegance and has elevated homemaking to a fine art. Instead of seeing this as the ultimate manner in which things *could* be done, however, some perfectionists have internalized her experience and craft as how they *should* be done. Even if you are not a Martha fan, see if you can find some relief in our twelve-step program:

The Twelve-Step Program of "Overdoers Anonymous."

1. We admit that our lives have become unmanageable trying to do it all.

2. We have come to believe that lowering our unrealistic standards can restore us to sanity.

3. We have made a decision to reduce the number and frequency of activities for ourselves and for our children.

4. We have made a searching and fearless inventory of our day planners.

5. We admitted to our families and friends that we can't possibly keep this up long term, and we have donated our superhero capes to charity.

6. We are entirely ready to buy a birthday cake from the supermarket and give up growing the pumpkin patch for autumn decor.

7. We have humbly asked ourselves for forgiveness for not being perfect and not being all things to all people.

8. We have made a list of tasks we can delegate and people with whom we can share driving duties.

9. We have made direct amends to people we have harmed wherever possible, especially ourselves.

10. We have continued to take personal inventory of our schedules and stopped ourselves from mindlessly volunteering.

11. We have sought to improve our conscious decisions about why and how we are spending our time every day and outsource tasks whenever it makes sense for our families and ourselves.

12. Having had an awakening as the result of these steps, we try to carry this message to others and pass it on to our children.

This twelve-step addiction "program" is just a joke, but the message is not. Are you addicted to excessive activity? When you're quietly alone with your thoughts, do you enjoy your own company? Why are you so busy? It's something to think and journal about.

For some great time-saving ideas, we have a free 12-page report called *30 Ways to Find Time to Get Organized,* available along with our wallet reminder sleeves when you sign up for our weekly newsletter. Go to www.clutterdiet.com/book to read more.

Communication Clutter

The second category of "invisible clutter" is communications, like e-mails and calls. These time-wasting items may be just sound waves in the air or stored on a server somewhere, but they clog the flow of your life and waste your time just as much as physical clutter does on your countertops.

Junk e-mail, or spam, is of course the worst culprit. As a business owner, I can't even begin to tell you how much time I have wasted dealing with problems caused by spammers. Make sure that you have a good spam filter in place, both at the server level (usually done by your e-mail service provider) and on the user level (such as filters inside Outlook that filter messages after they arrive in your inbox).

Unnecessary e-mails are more difficult to ascertain. Do you really need the weekly "best airfare deals" sent to you when you only travel once a year? Do you really need to stay on someone's mailing list forever after you buy from them once? Sometimes there are great reasons to keep receiving messages like these, but if you find yourself constantly deleting a certain type of message because you never read it, you probably should unsubscribe (*not*

to MY newsletter, though!). Pay attention to this for a week or so and start diligently unsubscribing to things you don't read or that you find annoying. It takes a few more seconds than just deleting, but you save all that time later when you no longer receive the messages.

If you use Outlook, one of my favorite things to do is use "Rules" to help you manage your mail better, with techniques like color-coding and automatic sorting. Click on a message of the type you'd like to color-code, such as a message from a certain address. Then choose Tools>Organize. There you'll see a menu where you can choose "Using Colors." Apply the settings you'd like for that situation, such as messages from a certain person or address being colored red or blue. You can also create rules with more advanced settings with the Tools>Rules and Alerts menu, where you can choose criteria like certain words in the subject line. Experiment with creating new rules (I always like to start with a blank rule) to have emails automatically sent to a certain folder when they arrive, make a certain type of e-mail automatically forward to another person, or display a special alert.

I have particularly appreciated using Outlook Rules when I am transitioning from an old e-mail address to a new one. If you color-code all of the messages sent to your old address, you can quickly see which people are still sending to that address and remind them in your reply to start using the new one.

Next to spam, telemarketing calls are one of the biggest annoyances and time-wasters on the planet, hands down! There are a couple of strong ways to combat them: First, have a strict personal policy of what to say when they call, and second, always use the tactic of asking to be removed from their list.

Have you ever been in a store to return something and the clerk tells you they cannot accept your return for a silly reason, but it's "just policy?" The clerk can hide behind the rule of policy and feel like he's not the "bad guy." Well, you can do that too! Make a personal policy agreement with yourself that you will not buy from, accept, or donate to anything offered or requested in a phone solicitation. *There, you've already decided!* Now you can say you "have a policy," which is easier than making a decision on each call's proposed offer.

You might say that you have Caller ID service, so you just won't answer the phone. I would argue that it's important to answer anyway, because you can invest just one minute to ask to be removed from their list, and that will prevent future calls from occurring. So do talk to them, apply your "strict policy," and then always take that extra moment before hanging up to ask to be removed from their list.

The law is now more on your side in telemarketing matters, as you can place all of your telephone numbers on the government "do not call" lists.

The U.S. Federal Trade Commission's National Do Not Call Registry:
www.donotcall.gov
State Do Not Call Directory:
www.callcompliance.com/regulations/statelist.html
Canadian National Do Not Call List:
https://www.lnnte-dncl.gc.ca

The telemarketers are required to cross-check their lists against this registry and are not allowed to call you. The websites provide more information about your particular rights and remedies.

Don't fall for the trap of receiving additional materials in the mail or getting something for free! While writing this book I received a call from my local newspaper, from whom I take a weekend-only subscription. They offered to give me the weekday paper free for a whole year, and it would have been tempting except for two things: 1) I have a personal policy that I do not respond to phone solicitations, and 2) I know that even a free daily newspaper will sit unread for the entire week and create new stacks of clutter that we will need to recycle. You'll often get offers like these that are not asking for money but they want to verify your address to send you something, or they want to sign you up for a few free months of an additional service like credit protection on your account. It might be free initially, but then you'll have to remember to cancel later, so make sure that you don't let them sign you up in the first place. Be assertive but polite, asking them to not send you anything and making sure they understand that you are not going to take their offer.

Having policies and being assertive works wonders to reduce or even eliminate the clutter of these unwanted calls!

But what about "friendly fire"—the calls that you actually enjoy but are still stealing your time away? Prolonged chats on the phone are another form of communication clutter. Remember that *you* are in control of how much time you spend on the phone! You have the option of whether and when to answer your phone, and you certainly have the option to cut conversations short when needed.

If you like chatting on the phone, make that a reward (a "dessert!") for yourself, and try to do something productive like folding laundry or cleaning out the refrigerator while you chat. Getting a headset will be a great liberating idea for you if you enjoy chatting! Another strategy is to give yourself a time limit and set a timer. You can even joke about it and be up front about it with your friends. "Oops, my time is up! I have to make myself get back to my work!"

If the problem is more about your friends or business associates wanting to talk longer and you don't, you may need to get more assertive about ending the call. It's really okay to say that you have another call to make, another appointment to attend, or another place you need to be. If you need to call people like these, plan your call in advance. According to Stephen Young, a time management consultant, an unplanned telephone call takes an average time of twelve minutes, but a planned call takes up an average of only seven minutes. So a savings of five minutes is possible for every call if you plan it before dialing!

Clutter Fitness Exercise

What strategies can you implement right away to reduce your Time & Communication clutter? Write down three things on which you will take action or change this week.

Devoting a little of
yourself to everything
means committing a
great deal of yourself
to nothing.

– Michael LeBoeuf

Reduction

Losing Clutter-Pounds!

Now that you've gotten motivated and starting thinking about the prevention of all kinds of clutter, you need to start reducing what has already accumulated in your home. In this section of the book, in your Clutter Fitness Workbook, you're going to be planning the projects which will help you start losing Clutter-Pounds!

As you go through your home doing organizing projects, you will need to have a plan for how to deal with unwanted items, as they have a tendency to reabsorb themselves into your home! So let's go over the five options you have for disposing of items you don't want or need.

1. Toss It

Obviously, some things are going to be simply *trash*. You'll probably have a lot of it! Later in this section of the book we'll cover the best trash bags and other tools to make dealing with the disposal easier.

Classifying something as trash may seem evident to you, but in working with our clients we find people have varied definitions of what constitutes "trash." Anything in these categories is most likely trash, and you'd have to do some fast talking to get me to think otherwise:

- Torn
- Stained
- Threadbare
- Shrunken
- Bleach-spotted
- Unraveling
- "Hole-y" (and I don't mean religious!)
- Rotten

- Outdated
- Used up
- Contaminated
- Smelly
- Moldy or mildewed
- Bug-infested
- Rusty

If you think that items in some of these categories might still be okay to donate, don't. Charity organizations do not accept things that can't be successfully re-used by someone else, and that means considering the normal use for the item. In other words, a t-shirt that is stained and torn is unable to be worn by someone, and although it's true that you could use it for stuffing a pillow or for a cleaning rag, that is not what the charity wants.

Shredding

Practice safe disposal! Shredding is more important than ever with identity theft being one of the fastest growing crimes. We recommend that every household have a shredder, and that you purchase one that shreds a minimum thickness of eight sheets at a time, preferably more. Think about one envelope with two sheets of paper folded inside it—the two pages folded into thirds make six thicknesses of paper. If you count the two thicknesses of the envelope holding it, that is a total of eight sheets. If you've already identified that you want to shred something, you will want to be able to stick the envelope directly into the shredder without opening it.

You should buy a name-brand shredder of high quality, as shredders tend to break easily. Mark my words; you will be frustrated if you get a cheap shredder that clogs! It's an investment, like an insurance policy against crime. I like buying shredders that also have the ability to shred CDs and DVDs safely, since our electronic data is sensitive. Shredder blades do need to be oiled, and you can buy special shredder oil for this purpose, but instead I like the shredder oiling sheets that you just feed through periodically. These sheets are much neater than their liquid counterpart and are simple to put through after you've just shredded a large batch of paper.

What should you shred? Err on the side of caution; in other words, it's better to shred too much than too little. Shred anything you are disposing that has financial information on it, account numbers, personal identification information or medical information. We always say to shred anything that would damage your identity, your finances, your privacy or your reputation!

If you have a big backlog of shredding to do, such as multiple boxes full of old papers in your garage, a document management company in your hometown likely has a mobile shredding truck that can come to your home

and do the shredding onsite. My preference is for those trucks that grind up your paper in front of a camera mounted inside the truck itself, while you watch on the monitor they have. Watching this is actually quite interesting. Your paper gets chewed up into giant rotating Dudley-Do-Right villain blades. You witness the shredding yourself and they give you a "Certificate of Destruction" right on the spot, which makes you feel secure about parting with the information. I have done this many times with clients, and one of the most satisfying parts of this experience is the immediate loss of Clutter-Pounds! Each container the technicians load on the trucks we use holds 300 pounds of paper, so my clients lose hundreds of Clutter-Pounds in about 30 minutes!

Clearly a mobile shredding truck is the most secure and convenient way to handle your confidential documents, but if that is not available in your area or your street is not accessible to the truck, there are other ways to get it done. The second most secure way is to bring the papers yourself to a shredding company's location and observe the destruction there. If you want a convenient option and are not as worried about witnessing the destruction, the shredding companies will typically be able to send a truck to pick up your documents and securely transport them to their location to destroy them.

Ask the shredding company if there are restrictions on what they will accept. The shredding trucks we use will even grind up old floppy disks and CDs, and it's okay to put hanging folders through with the metal braces in them. But your shredder may have a different policy regarding these items, so ask if you are not sure.

Keep your ears open for a free community shredding event in your area. Shredding companies commonly will provide a "drive-through" shredding experience once or twice a year as part of a bigger citywide promotion of some kind, like Earth Day, for example. Usually they have a limit on how many boxes or pounds they will accept per household, so do check this detail before driving your boxes over there.

Get Your Greens!

Recycling is obviously another subset of disposal, and the availability of recycling services unfortunately varies widely depending upon your location. Many cities now have at least curbside paper recycling for their residents. You'll need to contact your local waste disposal service to find out exactly what they take, and if you have a larger amount than your normal weekly pickup, ask them what they would prefer for bundling it up. For example, if you have more cardboard than will fit into your recycling bin, your service may want it to be flattened and bundled with twine.

You may also have more recycling options in your city that are available only if you drive your items over to their collection sites. Search online for your city plus the word recycling, or visit your city government's website for their list of resources.

Beware: Dangerous Trash

Hazardous waste disposal is a serious concern because of the accumulated effects of every household's relatively small contribution to the overall contamination. According to Ohio State University, if every household in a city of 50,000 supplies an average of five gallons of hazardous material to the environment each year, that equals more than 250,000 gallons or roughly 41 tons per year! From the Earth911.org website, here are the four main categories of household hazardous waste:

Automotive Products: motor oil, brake and transmission fluid, antifreeze and car batteries, gasoline, kerosene, diesel fuel, car wax with solvent and windshield wiper fluid.

Home Improvement Products: paint, varnish, stain, paint thinner, paint stripper, caulk, adhesives, primer, rust remover, turpentine, mineral spirits and glues.

Household Cleaners: drain cleaners, oven cleaners, toilet cleaners, spot removers, silver polishes, furniture polishes, window cleaners, bleach, dyes, tub and tile cleaner and ammonia.

Pesticides: insecticide and insect repellant, weed killer, rat and mouse poison, pet spray and dip, flea collars, mothballs, ant/roach killer, garden fungicides, slug poison, wood preservative and banned pesticides.

Other household hazardous products that don't fit into these categories include certain electronics, batteries, aerosol products, air fresheners, smoke detectors, shoe polish, cosmetics, pool chemicals, lighter fluid, prescription medicines and arts and craft materials.

Your city probably has a hazardous waste disposal facility where residents can drop off their household chemicals like the ones listed above, or they may organize a community drop off day during the year. Search online for "hazardous waste disposal" plus the name of your city, or you can visit Earth911.org and search for a resource for the specific chemical or item.

Once you're aware of the impact of hazardous waste, it makes a lot of sense not to buy it in the first place. If there is an environmentally-friendly, non-toxic alternative for your needs, consider the environment in your purchasing decision, and factor in the time it will take you to properly dispose of the item later.

As you're doing organizing projects, especially garages and sheds, make sure that you centralize all of the hazardous waste materials into one box for easier handling when it's time to take them away.

IMPORTANT: One Final Word about Recycling

With all of the options available to recycle or donate specific items like old cellular phones, batteries, mattresses, athletic shoes, computers, and the like, it's easy to fall into the trap of finding that "PERFECT" recycling option for each thing and then end up stuck making those decisions with the items still stored in your house. Remember that procrastination is the root cause of almost all clutter, so avoid putting up obstacles that make it more difficult to remove unwanted items from your home! At some point it's better to donate all the items to one place instead of parsing each item out to its own perfect home. Really, it's okay. You need to be free of it.

2. Give It to Friends

The next option for disposing of unwanted items is to give them to family or friends. As you're doing your organizing projects, if you have specific friends in mind, make a special box or bag for each one so you can quickly sort your items into them.

You'll want to have a strategy in place for the successful transfer of these items to the lucky person. Here are some options for making sure you don't store the items any longer than necessary:

- **Identify a time when you are going to see that person and write a note on your calendar to remember to bring his or her "new stuff" with you.** If the time is drawing near, put the items in your car so you won't forget them.

- **Have them pick it up from you.** Give them a deadline to do this if you feel it may be a problem for you to wait too long.

- **Ship it to them.** Many neighborhoods have a "pack and mail" store that will quickly and easily take care of these needs.

Don't be offended if your friends and family don't want to take your disposed belongings off your hands, and accept their "no" without insisting. Remember, one person's disposal is another person's "Acquired Clutter!" If they don't want it, you can take our next option…

3. Give It to Others

Working as a Professional Organizer for so many years, I most certainly have the Salvation Army and other charities on speed dial! **Identifying a nonprofit organization that will pick up directly from your home is a great idea, because waiting to take items yourself sometimes gets procrastinated (imagine that).** Ideally you can call them when you're starting a big project and schedule a pickup for a few days later. Doing this gives you additional accountability to get the project finished, too!

If you can't find a charity that has pick-up service, load everything up and take it in your car right away. Make sure you do this quickly after the project's complete so you don't change your mind about any of the items and so that they don't continue to clutter your life.

Freecycle.org is a great resource for giving things away, especially when you really want specific items to "find a good home." Someone I know had a television to give away and requested that people write to her saying why they wanted the TV. She was able to choose from the people who wrote in and ultimately gave it to the only person who didn't actually have a television yet. All of the other applicants wanted to use it for a second or third set, and she felt great about helping exactly the right person who really needed it.

Readers in the U.S. should make sure when donating items to a nonprofit organization, that they get a receipt for tax purposes. You can use our free Itemized Donations List form, found on our website at <u>www.clutterdiet.com/ freetips</u>, to capture information easily about your donation, then use the great valuation tool at <u>www.itsdeductibleonline.com</u> to assign values to your items. You'll be surprised how much your stuff is worth! For example, can you believe that frumpy bridesmaid dress in the back of your closet (in excellent condition) has a fair market value of $22.00? Organizing really pays off.

4. Return It

During your organizing projects you will almost always run across items that need to be returned, either to a friend, a store or library. In our *Room by Room Recipes* section we describe setting up a "Destination Station" with an Errand Shelf. The Errand Shelf is the ideal place to put your items to be returned, or you can put them into your car. Either way make sure to write down the errand itself on your task list so it will get done. You may even get some money back, or at least store credit, so that fact could be quite motivating.

5. Sell It

Money talks! If your unwanted items are saying, "Sell me," you have numerous choices for getting some cold hard cash. This is yet another way that organizing really pays.

- **Consignment stores.** Nicer clothing, especially children's clothes, costumes, formalwear and business suits, are terrific for consignment. Consignment stores that specialize in children's clothing may also accept toys, and many cities have furniture consignment stores that will even take decorative accessories. Read about the stores' policies online or call them to ask questions before just showing up with your stuff. You might find that you don't agree with how they operate, and there may be a better fit for your item elsewhere.

- **Craigslist.org.** My favorite option for selling items locally, or even elsewhere. I once bought some red cola glasses on Craigslist from someone in Detroit for a talent show where we needed to have them for the American Idol-style judges…proving that you can find almost anything you want and certainly can sell anything too. Good ol' Craig's website has become the go-to place for the old-fashioned want-ad, and it's free!

- **eBay.com.** If you have a special, even collectible, item, eBay is definitely the best place to sell it. You can sell almost anything on eBay, very much like Craigslist, but there is a fee once your item has sold. The format is selling by auction instead of directly purchasing the items (although some sellers do offer the "Buy It Now" choice too). If you are intimidated by setting up the auctions yourself, you can ask someone in your neighborhood for help, as I am sure there is a whiz kid within reach who will be glad to list your wares. There are also a number of eBay stores around the country that will sell things on eBay for you and take a percentage on commission. One successful chain is called I Sold It, found at www.i-soldit.com. They have stores across the United States and some in Canada and Australia. A newer option is Zippi.com, with a network of eBay sellers who will pick up your items from your home and sell them for you.

- **Yard sales.** Typically I do not recommend having a yard sale, unless you really like doing it. It is extremely time-consuming and tiring to prepare for it, set up the sale, promote it well, monitor it, negotiate with buyers all day on a weekend, and take everything down when you're finished. At the end of a yard sale you usually make the one trip you might have already done anyway—driving the remainder to your favorite charity. A tax deduction on that donation is usually a better use of most people's time and energy. However, if you insist, there are some resources online with great tips, such as YardSaleQueen.com and WeekendTreasure.com. You can get supplies for your sale at YardSaleSupplies.com.

How to Track Your Clutter-Pounds

With these five different kinds of disposal going on, you'll most likely be losing tons of Clutter-Pounds! Some people really enjoy competing with themselves and setting numerical goals, and if you think that will motivate you, here are some optional ways to track how many "C-Lbs." you've lost from our program and your efforts:

Tracking Option 1: You can use the system we use on the Clutter Diet website. It's not exact by any means, but it's a fun way of tracking your progress and it's easier than the second choice below.

One large black lawn & leaf bag full of trash = 5 Clutter-Pounds

1 book or produce box, or 1 large shopping bag full of donation items = 5 Clutter-Pounds

We also give Clutter-Pounds credit for doing our weekly project plans:

Main Dish = 10 Clutter-Pounds

Side Dishes = 5 Clutter-Pounds

Sensible Snack = 2 Clutter-Pounds

Dessert = 2 Clutter-Pounds (Note that we give credit for rewarding yourself. It's that important!)

Tracking Option 2: You can literally weigh everything that is leaving your house! Some clients and members have done this just because they really wanted to know how many pounds of stuff they had shed from their lives. To do this you'd need an inexpensive shipping scale that displays the numbers separately from the main weighing unit, as putting a large garbage bag on your normal bathroom scale makes it nearly impossible to read the numbers.

Again, this is optional and just for fun if you like having statistical ways to track your progress. If you want to enroll in the Clutter Diet program, you can easily "weigh-in" each week with the weekly plan of projects we provide, and your cumulative Clutter-Pounds total is displayed each time you log in to the member area.

Clutter Fitness Exercises

- Think of one to three items in your home you already know you need to return. What are they? Can you commit to returning at least one within a specific time frame? Ask your Motivation Partner if he or she has similar things to return—you might even be going to the same places!

- Are there pricier items that you need to sell, such as nice formal wear or high-end electronics? Find out the resources for selling in your area.

- Is there someone in your neighborhood or at work who might be able to help you list items for sale online? Talk to that person and set a time to get together.

- It's a good idea to make a Disposal Plan as a future reference for you to follow as you tackle your organizing projects. When you're finished organizing, you want to be free and clear of the debris as soon as possible so you can enjoy the results, and your Disposal Plan can make that happen. Write your plan directly into your Clutter Fitness Workbook, available at www.clutterdiet.com/book.

My Disposal Plan

Trash:

My normal curbside trash pickup day(s): _____

_____

_____

(Depending upon your needs, it may be beneficial to schedule your organizing projects around your pickup days.)

Name and phone number of my waste disposal company:

_____

_____

_____

_____

_____

My trash service picks up large items like mattresses at the following times:

_____

_____

_____

_____

_____

Local hazardous waste disposal information:

_____

_____

_____

_____

_____

_____

_____

Recycling:

Guidelines for accepting (note exactly what types are accepted, especially paper and plastic):

• Paper: _____
_____

• Plastics: _____
_____

• Steel Cans: _____
_____

• Aluminum Cans: _____
_____

• Other: _____
_____

Recycling drop off locations and phone numbers:
_____
_____
_____
_____

Other notes:

Giving to Friends/Family

List friends and family members to whom you might want to give some of your belongings, noting what kinds of things they might like to have.

Key question: *ARE YOU SURE they want these items?*

Friend/Family Members

Items They May Want

Donations:

Name of favorite charitable organization and phone number:

_____ ❑ Does pickups

_____ ❑ Does pickups

_____ ❑ Does pickups

_____ ❑ Does pickups

_____ ❑ Does pickups

_____ ❑ Does pickups

Notes on acceptable items and pickup guidelines:

_____

_____

_____

_____

_____

_____

_____

_____

_____

_____

_____

Don't know some of this information? Use friends, Google or the phone book to help you find out. Make sure you take action to get the information you need.

Important SpaceScaping® Concepts

I coined and trademarked the term "SpaceScaping®" many years ago when searching for a verb to describe what we do as organizers. Yes, we organize, "declutter" and clean up spaces. But none of these words are quite descriptive enough of the actual process. SpaceScaping encompasses all of the following actions:

- Analyzing needs for items and space
- Organizing physical items
- Purging unnecessary items
- Storing belongings appropriately
- Maximizing available space
- Creating systems that work long term

This section of the book teaches you the SpaceScaping concepts that enable you to think like a Professional Organizer. At this point you are probably thinking heavily about those cluttered spaces in your home, wondering where to start and how to tackle this "Reduction" phase of the program. Let's start by looking at the most common reasons why a space is not working, so you can analyze your needs and approach your projects with the right strategy. Do any of these problems sound familiar?

"Boneless" Spaces

Your body needs a skeleton to hold it up, and a room needs a skeleton to hold its stuff! When there is no infrastructure in a room, no shelving or cabinets, there is no place for the stuff except for flat surfaces like the floor or tables.

We see these "boneless" spaces most often in garages and basements. Garages need shelving and cabinets because they are primarily for storage—that really is a garage's entire purpose. Without a skeleton of storage, things pile up around the periphery on the floor (the only flat surface available), they quickly spread into the center of the space, and the garage becomes unmanageable.

You'll want to go vertical to get your stuff off of the flat surfaces. Use the walls! Put up shelving, and if you already have shelves, could you add another one? We usually try to take shelving up as high as it can go, and we always try to get adjustable shelving if possible. Use hooks and racks too, for going vertical. If you have a television taking up space on a flat surface, mount it on the wall, whether it's a flat screen or you need to buy an older mounting arm for it. Think about what you could do to clear as much flat surface as possible for other things.

The furniture you choose is also part of the room's skeleton. Versatility and function are the winning features when shopping for furniture. Buy pieces that have multiple uses and ideally have storage in every possible nook and cranny. Sometimes people want to use a beautiful dining table for a desk, which looks nice, but then you have no drawers for storage! Remember, "form follows function," so consider your needs for function and storage first before going strictly for aesthetics.

Storage that is not working is almost as bad as not having it at all, so make sure you buy good quality furniture, shelving, and cabinets. A good example of this is squeaky, stuck file drawers. Who wants to file anything if you have to wrestle with the drawers just to get them open? Invest in quality pieces that will last and grow with you over the years. Buying on the cheap often makes you frustrated and ultimately wastes your money and time.

"Overweight" Spaces

Sometimes it's just this simple: You have too much stuff in the space. No matter how we slice it, any room or storage space can hold only a certain capacity, and if there is more, it simply won't fit. A closet is great example of an overweight space, as there is only so much linear rod space for clothes to hang. You can get special hangers and try a few other "tricks" to fit more clothing in, but at a certain point, you won't be able to fit one more hanger in, and you certainly won't be able to slide the clothing aside to view it and make your choices.

The cure for overweight spaces is to pare down the contents and prioritize what is most important to keep. You may need to overflow a portion of the contents into another space, like moving your out-of-season clothing to another closet.

"Clutter Cemetery"

Most homes have at least one place, like the garage, basement, guest room or attic, where things "go to die." You could also call these spaces "The Final Frontier" for your clutter. It's the place where, if you can't make a decision, you have just "put it there for now," and it has wasted away from then on.

To clear out a Clutter Cemetery, you need to focus heavily on decision-making. It's time for some "tough love" with some of those unused things that are weighing down your life. A good rule of thumb is to discard anything you have not used in one year, or if your current year has been a strange and atypical one, make it two. In Clutter Cemetery situations you will need to make good use of your disposal plan, so make sure you're ready with resources to quickly get rid of what you've decided to purge.

"Stressed Out" Spaces

In the next chapter we'll be going over how to analyze the functions of a room. **If there are too many major functions in the room, if there are too many things going on in the space, it will be difficult to accommodate them all adequately.** Something's got to give to make the room work.

We often see Stressed Out Spaces with spare bedrooms. Each family member may have a different idea for how to use the space, and the family tries to create a multi-purpose room to make everyone happy. Here are some of the major functions we commonly see trying to co-exist in one tiny bedroom:

- Home office
- Craft room
- Guest room
- Sewing room
- Scrapbooking room
- Reading nook
- Playroom
- Exercise room
- Recreation room
- Home theater
- Art studio
- Meditation space

Now imagine taking any three (or more) of these and making them operate in one small room. The arts-and-crafts-related functions may have a chance at working together, but trying to fit a treadmill and weight machine into a home office and leaving enough room also to do scrapbooking projects will be too much.

Room dividers like screens and shelving units can sometimes be effective at separating the space, but typically only if there are two major functions occurring and the room is not too small. You may need to move the excess functions to other rooms, or even give up the idea of that activity being in your home. We've seen clients who have downsized in a move, sold their treadmill or other exercise equipment and started going to a gym instead.

"Shared Custody" or Neglected Spaces

You just organized the pantry and you are so happy and satisfied with your work that you keep going back to the pantry just to admire it and sigh lovingly! You love being able to see what you have, enjoying the extra space there available to put new items, and not seeing lots of extraneous things in your pantry that don't belong. But after a few weeks or a couple of months, your pantry is getting close to the way it was before. What happened? Your kids went into the pantry each day for their snacks, and they didn't put things back where they belonged. They left lids off, didn't close up boxes and bags, and left empty packages there that should have been thrown away. Your spouse came home from the grocery store and just stashed the new items in the pantry without noticing where they should have been stored. These habits repeated over weeks or months wreak havoc with the system you created...in other words, they ruined your good work!

Often the "shared custody" of a space causes this frustrating deterioration. If the organizing systems are not communicated to others via labeling, procedures, signs, orientation or training, the people who were not involved in creating the systems may not understand or want to maintain them.

Of course your kids may not be old enough to understand your systems and there is a certain amount of tolerance you will have to show with children who don't take care of a space the same way that you would. That said, however, you can take a kid's point of view to make sure that you create systems that are as easy as possible to maintain.

Just remember a simple Spanish word, VEO. It means "I see." For our purposes, it represents the goals of creating an effective and lasting organizing system:

Visible: Your system should make whatever items you are organizing as visible as possible. You find things when you can see them. If it's clothing, organize it by type and by color, so you can easily see how many purple skirts you have. If it's food in your pantry, it should be organized by type and then not stacked up so deep that you can't see what's behind the front row of cans or boxes.

Easy: Your system should be easy to maintain. Whenever possible, use open baskets and bins without lids, because having a lid means one more step is required to put something away, and two hands are required instead of simply tossing something in. And if you are designing a pantry around a large set of matching containers with the intention of always putting new packages of food into them and discarding the original packaging, that approach will require an extra step after you unpack your groceries from the car.

Obvious: A system that is easy to maintain is obvious to everyone in terms of how to maintain it. If there is a label on a bin that says "Rice & Beans," it's clear that rice and beans go there and not candy. If your cookbooks are all sorted together in a row, it's obvious that cookbooks go on that shelf.

I mentioned orientation and training, and this may sound formal and businesslike, but it only takes a couple of minutes to show the people sharing the space what you've done and tell them what their part is in maintaining it. If you really want the best systems possible, get their input before starting the project. Point out to your family, for example, that there are now labels, and those are signs to show us where things should be stored. Explain that there is now a trash can or recycling bin near the pantry to throw away empty containers.

Ownership is a huge part of the problem in the "Shared Custody" of a space. When there isn't clarity on ownership of the maintenance, everyone thinks someone else is going to do it and it simply doesn't get done. Assign tasks and responsibilities so that the ownership is clear.

And if it's just you using the space, but it's been neglected, it's possible that you have made the maintenance for the space overcomplicated, or that you simply are not doing it. Your Motivation Partner's accountability might be just the right tool to help you get that maintenance done.

"Diagnosing" Your Space

Your space could be, in theory, a combination of any (or even all) of these "diagnoses." Seeing what is going wrong in a space helps you make it right, so it's important to think through this when outlining your plan. I cannot say this enough! Thinking through the diagnosis helps you get to the root of the problem in the space, and it's what makes the difference between "taking a stab at" organizing something and having a true professional approach. We'll be covering in detail how to outline a plan in the next chapter.

Clutter Fitness Exercises

- **It's time to get serious about your Motivation Partner.** If you don't have one, why not? If you have not asked someone to be your partner, do that *now*. This person could be also interested in getting organized, but he or she does not have to be on the same path as you. Maybe your potential partner has a different kind of goal to achieve, like writing a thesis. All that matters is that you hold each other accountable for your own specific goals.

- **If you already have a Motivation Partner, TERRIFIC!** The next step is to finalize with your partner a regular time to check in with each other each week, or if you prefer, each day. How will you check in, by phone or by e-mail?

- Go to the **SpaceScaping® Project Worksheet in your Clutter Fitness Workbook, found at <u>www.clutterdiet.com/book</u>.** If you've already decided what organizing project you'd like to do first, write down what you think the "diagnosis" is for this space. If you have not already decided what project you'd like to do first, keep reading, and we're going to explore the question of "Where Should I Start?" later in this section of the book.

How to Approach Your Projects

Many unsuccessful organizing projects have been started by "diving in" without thinking through the space. Our SpaceScaping® O.R.D.E.R. acronym provides the correct approach for almost any organizing project, whether it's a filing system, a closet, a chemistry lab or a garage. My team and I have used this approach for every project we have taken on with our clients, and now you can benefit from this model in your own home and life.

The most important part, as I have said, is outlining the plan first. Sometimes this planning requires objectivity, and you may have lost yours. You have probably been looking at the space too long. You have been living in it and contributing to its current state, and the contents have begun to look like "wallpaper" to you—just part of the scenery.

To gain the objectivity you need on your project, you could, of course, hire a professional to help you, or try some of these ideas:

- **Take photographs of the space.** Somehow that gives you a new perspective on a room. From a photograph you may realize things you don't notice when you're in the space in person. I have definitely had this experience, thinking, "Wow, I really need to hang something on that blank wall!" You will be surprised how photos make you step back from everyday living and see your space as others might see it for the first time.

- **Have a friend visit the space and help you go over the questions in the Outline Your Plan section below.** Ideally this person could be your Motivation Partner, but that's not required or even always possible. You just need someone who doesn't live in the space with you to give you a fresh pair of eyes.

- **Post your photos in our member area and get advice from our team of organizing experts.** Paid members can get our expert take on the situation seven days a week.

Put your Sherlock Holmes hat on. You are a detective and a problem solver! Now take your fresh perspective and apply it to our SpaceScaping® O.R.D.E.R. approach:

Outline Your Plan
Review Your Items
Decide Where Things Belong
Establish Homes & Routines
Revisit Your System

Outline Your Plan

Diagnosis: Reflecting on our last chapter, ask yourself what is going on in this space. How did it get this way? Do you have a "boneless" room or a "shared custody" situation? There is no need for blame; we're just objectively looking at causes to get to the root of the problem. You can't prescribe medication very well if you don't know what the illness is, right?

The first question I always ask is, "Who is using this space?" This may seem obvious to you, but think through it anyway. There may be factors you have not considered regarding children, housekeepers or guests.

When Outlining Your Plan, you also want to look at the four "F's" of your room (yes, we have four "F" words!): Features, Function, Flow and Frequency.

- **Features:**
  What is the skeleton of the room? Which features are changeable and which are not? Notice the furniture, plumbing, walls, closets and doors. Think about everything differently... what if you removed a door and left a closet open? What if you had a different piece of furniture?

- **Function:**
  Another question we always ask is, "What functions are happening in this space?" Think about the functions you would *like* to happen here, such as exercising or studying, that you might want to add once the space is improved.

  Let's take the case of a normal utility room. You might be surprised at everything that is going on in that tiny room! There are all the steps in caring for your clothing (sorting, washing, drying, folding, and ironing), plus possibly pet care needs, recycling, and storage of utility and cleaning items for maintaining the house. Each of these functions needs a dedicated zone for its supplies and required space.

- **Flow:**
  How do these features and functions relate to each other? Are there any obvious patterns here? Are there any "logjams" where clutter seems to be aggregating? Why?

  The kitchen. mudroom or front entryway may have a logjam of clutter from people coming in and out of the house. You might notice the "chain of custody" of the items—where did they come from? Can you stop the inflow of new items in some way? If you can't stop it, can you create a better system to accommodate it?

- **Frequency:**
  How often do these functions occur and how important are they? If you exercise three times a week, the treadmill has earned its position in the room. If you exercise once or twice a year on that treadmill and otherwise use it to drape clothing over, it probably needs to go.

Throughout your analysis, use what I call "The 3-Year-Old Method." Just as a 3 or 4 year-old child can amaze you with a never-ending stream of repeated questions, you should ask over and over again, "Why? Why? Why?" Keep asking why until you get to the real answer! Ask about things you think are obvious. Ask about things you think are silly. Ask, ask, ask!

One of my commercial clients had a small kitchen area for many people to share for breaks and lunches. Much of the room was crowded with large water jugs for the water dispenser, both empty and full, and they were really infringing upon the space available. I asked her *why* she had the jugs there, and she said at first, "Because the water dispenser is there." And then I asked her again, "Why?" and she said, "Because it needs to be in the kitchen area near the sink and the coffee maker." So I asked, "Why?" again, and she replied, "Because we need to have purified water for the employees and visitors." Then I asked her again, "Why?" She replied,

"Because our tap water is terrible." There was the root of the problem! If the tap water is terrible, are there other ways to get purified drinking water that don't take up so much space? Well, yes. A reverse osmosis system installed under the sink with its own tap solved the problem, and it saved both space and money! The R.O. purifier cost less to install and maintain than having a service deliver those heavy, bulky jugs. The 3-Year-Old Method really paid off.

Take a look at your diagnosis and the "four F's" and synthesize what you've learned to make a plan for your room. Think of it as a puzzle you are solving. Do you still have that Sherlock Holmes hat on? Each function should fit into its own zone and all of the functions should flow together.

Don't worry if you don't know what to do exactly! Here's a secret: I often don't. Sometimes it takes wading into the project to create the best solutions. But having done your homework, with these functions all ascertained, you will feel the solution is rather obvious when it appears.

Our last question is, "Are there any obvious supplies needed?" Now this is where people can get in trouble. One of the biggest mistakes we see is people going out to buy all kinds of organizing supplies before they know what they need.

You can intelligently determine some items, however, that will most certainly be required. You may realize there is no "skeleton" and you really need some shelving for the space, or you may know that you'll need to hang up an ironing board and get some supplies for recycling needs. If you are really sure, you can measure carefully and purchase the supplies needed to get started.

Review Your Items

Now that you have a plan and you know what you are trying to accomplish in the room, you need to review the items that currently live there. *Where within the room do you start?* Here are a few strategies:

- **Circular:** Pick a spot near the door and sort thoroughly in a circular pattern around the room until you return to that spot.
- **Outside-In:** Start with flat surfaces like tables and countertops, then move to piles on the floor, then tackle whatever is inside cabinets.
- **Centralized:** Centralize everything first before sorting. For example, if you are organizing a bedroom, you might want to make the bed first and then go around the room gathering all clutter and throwing it all onto the bed. The room will then be clean, and you can just focus on the bed and sort from there.

Outline Your Plan
Review Your Items
Decide Where Things Belong
Establish Homes & Routines
Revisit Your System

Reviewing means sorting things into categories based on what makes sense. If you are organizing a sewing room and you are sorting thread, you might sort it by color, or by whether it's cotton or polyester thread. **There will almost always be multiple options for sorting something, but what you want ask is,** *"What is going to make it easier for me to find and manage these items later?"* Most often you'll want to sort by function, such as pet care supplies, recycling, laundry supplies, cleaning supplies, and so on. But you could also sort by anything else that makes sense for the situation, such as:

- Color
- Size
- Type
- Name/Alphabetical
- Owner
- Subject
- Date
- Stage or phase
- Potency or dosage
- Priority

Reviewing Caution #1: We refer to the Reviewing stage as the "Scary Phase." Everything is spread out, and you may even need to clear some space for a "staging area" to be able to do the sorting. Don't worry! Remember, visibility is crucial to the organizing process, and the only way to create this visibility and make better decisions about your stuff is to get it all out where you can see it and make your choices. It gets a little worse before it gets better, but *just keep going.*

Reviewing Caution #2: Your sorting session is meant to be fast and practical, *not a trip down memory lane.* If you are tempted to sit and reminisce, make that a reward for yourself after you've achieved a small goal in your project. If you are working with a partner, have that person keep you on task.

Reviewing Caution #3: "Elsewhere" items often appear while sorting, such as items that need to be returned and items that belong in another room like the kitchen or home office. Create a group of these Elsewhere items right where you are and keep going. Don't get distracted taking these things somewhere else and abandon your project. If there are many items, you can create subgroups based on where the items go to make putting them away easier later.

Decide Where Things Belong

Reviewing and sorting goes along concurrently with the next letter in our O.R.D.E.R. acronym, D for Decide. As you're sorting you'll be making decisions about your things.

When you really get down to the essence of our role as Professional Organizers, *we help people make decisions.* It's that simple. The root cause of clutter is procrastination of these decisions, and we help you bring them to the forefront and bust through them. **Being more organized in your life means being more decisive—about your stuff, your time and your information.**

Outline Your Plan
Review Your Items
Decide Where Things Belong
Establish Homes & Routines
Revisit Your System

One of the tools we use to help people make decisions is our A-B-C-D method of prioritization. We refer to things as A, B, C or D in terms of their frequency of use, and we refer to places as A, B, C or D in terms of their accessibility.

"A" things are used frequently, even daily or multiple times per day, like your toothbrush or your paper towels. "A" spaces are your countertops and other flat surfaces; the most eye-level, easy to reach shelves; the handiest drawers; and the other most easily accessible spaces in your home.

"B" things are used often but just not as frequently as the "A" things, like a blender or maybe a large salad bowl. They need to be put in "B" spaces, meaning behind "A" things, above or below "A" things, inside a cabinet or in otherwise less accessible spots.

Things	Priorities	Places
Pens, stapler, toothbrush, dishes	**A** Used frequently, even daily.	Handiest drawer or on top of desk/counter
3-hole punch, iron, blender	**B** Used often; weekly or monthly.	Above, below or behind "A" items, enclosed in cabinet
Holiday decorations	**C** Used rarely or seasonally.	Higher shelves, less accessible places—even attic
Archived documents, skis, spare furniture	**D** Never or seldom used.	Completely out of daily flow—in least accessible location or offsite storage

"C" things are used, but they are used infrequently or seasonally, such as holiday decorations. They need to be in "C" places that are less accessible and completely out of the way of the daily flow of living in your home. **"D" things are items you actually do not use, but you feel you have to keep them anyway, like old tax records or spare furniture.** Categorizing something as "D" does not automatically mean it's bad and should be discarded. There are good "D" things like memorabilia and baby clothes that are being saved for a future child. But "D" things need to be in "D" places, as out of the way as possible. Of course, we encourage you to think carefully about discarding "D" things, since by definition you are not using them.

People always joke with us that they have "E" and "F" things, but everything you own really does fit in this model somewhere. This A-B-C-D prioritizing tool is a useful way of thinking and talking about your stuff, and it quickly helps you decide how you're using something and where it should be. **The goal is to get the "A" things in the "A" places, and the "D" things in the "D" places.** We see all the time things that are "C" things in "A" places, and so on, taking up valuable real estate in your space.

During this phase of reviewing and deciding, it's helpful to ask yourself some questions when you are unsure about an item. Here are some of our favorites:

- **When is the last time you used this item?** If it's been more than a year, it's unlikely that you will use it again. (Make it two years if you must, but set a time frame and stick to it.) If you're not sure and can't make a decision, you can mark the item with a note indicating the date, and during a future project you can see how long it's been since you reviewed and decided upon it before. If you have lots of small items like these, bundle them together in one box and seal it up with the date on the outside.

- **What is a scenario in which you can actually see yourself using it, and how likely is that to happen?** Sometimes people say "I might need it someday," and we ask them this question. We've gotten some ridiculous and hilarious answers. A client here in Austin had a fur coat that she hadn't worn in ten years, and when she did travel to snowy and cold regions, she never wanted to pack it along. She finally cooked up a scenario about needing it someday if a blizzard were to hit Central Texas. We both got a good laugh out of that one and decided to sell the coat on consignment.

- **What does it cost (in both time and money) to replace this item? And how hard would it be to find and purchase this item again?** Sometimes you haven't used something in a long time and are keeping it "just in case," when in reality it is easily replaced if you need it again. Is the item worth taking up your valuable "A" and "B" space if it's not really an "A" or "B" item in terms of frequency?

- **What is the worst case scenario if you did get rid of this item?** The answer to this question might not be so bad, and just the act of stopping to consider it makes things obvious.

The bottom line is that you need to make room in your life for your "A" and "B" items and really think hard about anything else you don't use as often.

During this Reviewing and Deciding phase, you begin to accumulate various piles, which you will deal with during the later phases of the project:

- **Keep:** Various categories of items you'll be saving and storing here (Subcategories will based on how you're sorting, such as "pants," "blouses" or "socks." You also may have some action categories such as "repairs.")
- **Elsewhere:** Items that belong elsewhere in your home or another place, as well as returns
- **Trash:** Garbage and other kinds of disposal such as recycling and shredding
- **Donations/Give to Friend:** Items you are giving to charity or others
- **Sell:** Items for consignment stores, Craigslist, eBay or a garage sale

I'll say it again: Being more organized in your life means being more decisive—about your stuff, your time and your information. As you are Reviewing and Deciding about your things, make sure you are making decisions that support the person you are trying to be. Are you aligning your home to the goals you have for your life? Go back to your workbook and remind yourself of the compelling reasons you have for getting organized and your vision for what that will do for you.

You may run across possessions that bring up bad memories or feelings, so keep your vision in mind as you consider them. Does each item support you in your goals? I am not an expert in Feng Shui, loosely defined as the art of arranging your objects and furniture to help you achieve your goals and increase the flow of energy in your home. But I do know that it's "bad Feng Shui" to keep things that remind you of horrible memories. If there is a dress that you wore to your divorce hearing, every time you wear it you'll be thinking about that day. Giving it away means you'll no longer have those thoughts when you go to choose clothing in your closet.

Another final word about making decisions: **Usually indecisiveness is based in fear, since it means you are afraid of making "The Wrong Choice."** Keeping things you no longer need is almost always rooted in fear, as in, "I'm afraid I might need it someday/I won't be able to find that again/my daughter might need it/(fill in the blank with your own concerns)." Here is a two-word weapon for you in the fight against fear: **"SO WHAT?"** What if you might need it someday? So what? What if your daughter needs it? So what? Answer that question and plow forward. **Don't let fear stop you from creating the life you want!**

Establish Homes & Routines

Now that you've made decisions about your belongings and disposed of things you don't need, you can establish homes for them and routines for keeping the space maintained. In this phase we'll be choosing containers and making sure our systems are VEO—Visible, Easy, and Obvious.

Outline Your Plan
Review Your Items
Decide Where Things Belong
Establish Homes & Routines
Revisit Your System

Everything needs a home. If you've decided something is worth keeping, it deserves an established place of its own. Finding things later depends upon this concept! I sometimes have fun asking audiences if they know where their underwear is located. Almost everyone does have a home for their underwear, typically a certain drawer (a drawer for your drawers!). And most people know exactly where the milk is in the refrigerator, because there is a spot for that. Let's translate this concept to the rest of the items in your home, as much as possible.

One consideration for establishing a home for items is based on our A-B-C-D ideas, putting frequently used items in the most accessible spaces and so on. If you wear a pair of shoes only once a year with your formalwear, you'll want to put those shoes up high on a "C" shelf in a shoebox rather than having them on the floor next to your running shoes (an "A" space).

Another consideration for establishing homes is the "point-of-use." You'll want to put the dishtowels near the sink, and the pot holders near the stove. Where are you going to be when you need this item most? It's possible that duplicate items might be desirable when considering point-of-use. For example, you might have multiple pairs of scissors in your home for the office, the kitchen, and the gift wrapping supplies.

Be sure to consider safety during this phase, especially for children. When establishing homes for items, make sure to keep poisons, sharp objects, and other dangerous items out of kids' reach. Also make sure anything children will want to reach for themselves does not require any climbing. If you have doubts, secure bookcases to the wall so that a climbing child will not pull the shelves down on himself. A great resource for more information is my friend Alison Rhodes, "The Safety Mom," who has a special article for our readers on storage safety at www.safetymom.com/storage.

Labeling helps tremendously in establishing the home for an item. Here are a few favorite ways to label your stuff:

- **Sharpie® permanent markers.** We really like the retractable kind, because you don't have to fumble with a cap and potentially lose it, and it's a one-hand operation to click it open instead of a two-hand operation to pull the cap off. You can write directly on plastic and paper and almost anything else. We also love the metallic versions of these markers, as the silver ink shows up well on dark items. You can write directly onto a black videotape, for example.

- **Sharpie's Rub-A-Dub® laundry markers.** You can easily label clothing and fabrics with this indelible ink. We like marking children's clothing to make it effortless to sort and put away.

- **Label makers.** In the next chapter we will be discussing your Organizing Toolkit, and we'll talk about purchasing one. Affixing a printed label to your bins, shelves, and baskets is the best way to communicate the home for the items you're storing.

- **String tags.** When your label tape won't easily stick to the container's surface by itself, such as on a wicker basket, a round string tag is an attractive way to provide a labeling surface. I like the Avery 11031 Metal Rim String Tags, the 1-9/16" size. If you care about the aesthetics of the project you're doing, string the tag with a colorful ribbon instead of the provided white cotton string.

- **Binder clips.** I invented this idea for labeling while in the shower one day thinking about a solution to a challenging problem for a client! Medium black binder clips are extremely inexpensive and are available at any office supply store. Try this solution: print a label on your label maker and adhere it to the back of the binder clip, then clip it onto any very narrow edge such as a tray. Fold the chrome parts back out of the way, or just squeeze sideways to remove them, leaving only the black portion of the clip there.

- **Printable label sheets and label printers.** If you have multiple labels to print at once, choose a label sheet to run through your printer and format the labels in your word processing software. You can also buy a special printer that prints rolls of labels to have always at the ready.

- **Clear packing tape.** Sometimes you have a good representative piece of the original packaging of a toy or a food that you'd like to use as a label. Maybe it has a picture of the item on it, or important instructions you'd like to save. Simply cut it out and tape it to a new container. Clear packing tape allows you to adhere the paper to the container and also protects and reinforces the label.

5 Ways to Find Hidden Space

Are you out of space? Here are some tricks for finding more:

- **Go vertical.** Make sure you have maximized use of all your wall space and any wasted space between shelves. "Helper shelves" are accessories that provide one extra level of storage if you don't have adjustable shelving.

- **Don't forget the backs of doors.** Pantry and closet doors provide a large amount of space, and there are many products made just for them. Look up the word "overdoor" at sites like Organize.com or ContainerStore.com to see a large selection. Cabinet doors may also provide some storage options.

- **Go deep.** Make the most use of deep cabinets and corners by using turntables, also known as "lazy Susans." Glide-out shelves installed in lower cabinets are also terrific solutions for depth.

- **Hang from the ceiling.** Bike hoists are great for getting bicycles out of the way in the garage, and you can use hooks in your garage or pantry to hang lots of things like baskets and tools. Overhead racks for the garage are becoming popular, with many brands on the market providing what they call the "second attic."

- **Get radical.** Rip out that closet that is not serving your needs. If you use a spare bedroom as an office, a closet configuration with hanging rods for a wardrobe is not the right solution. Add several rows of adjustable shelving there to provide proper storage instead.

Choosing containers is also part of this stage. These choices are subjective, depending upon your personal style. I have had some clients who hate plastic, and others who don't care either way. Here are some considerations for making your choice:

- **Size:** Always measure your items and the space where the container will need to fit before purchasing your bins or baskets.
- **Aesthetics:** Do you need the containers to look nice? You may want them to be a certain color or material (like wicker or metal). If they don't need to look beautiful, you will have more options for both price and variety.
- **Visible vs. hidden:** Do you want to see the contents through a clear container, or do you want to hide the contents behind an opaque material? Clear containers are great whenever possible, as we know that visibility is an important factor in finding and managing your belongings.
- **Shape:** Square or rectangular containers use space much more efficiently than rounded containers.
- **Ease of use:** Do you need the container to have a lid, or is it better to have an open container? Would it be beneficial to have wheels on it? Take care that you choose something as easy as possible to use.
- **Ease of care:** If the container will need to be cleaned, consider its shape together with the contents in terms of the ease of cleaning it later. Does it have lots of grooves and crevices that might make that difficult? If it's fabric, is it washable?

I like shopping for containers and other organizing supplies at large discount stores like Target and Wal-Mart first, sometimes even "dollar" stores, and then moving on to specialty stores if I cannot find what I need. I also like import stores like Pier One or World Market for a great selection of attractive baskets. Clients have found great deals at their local thrift stores, like Goodwill. I got some excellent, large, red and green Christmas bins at

Goodwill myself one time, and I have seen furniture there such as small tables and storage pieces too.

Establishing routines is also part of this phase. You've created the homes for these items, but there is a system involved in maintaining it. What are the specific steps required to keep this area in good shape?

If you are organizing a utility room, those tasks might look like this:

- Put away clothing after it's hung and folded
- Take out the recycling
- Bring empty hangers here from closets
- Monitor supply of laundry and cleaning products and purchase when needed
- Clean room every other week

The next section of the book is about Maintenance, and we'll be talking about how to put those tasks into a workable plan to make sure someone takes care of the space and systems you've created. Take note of the specific tasks, even if you just think through them in your mind without writing them down, because they are crucial to the success of your project over time.

Revisit Your System

The final step in our O.R.D.E.R. process is to Revisit the systems you've created. Few things are perfect the first time. Most systems and spaces need a little tweaking here and there, particularly because life goes on and things do change.

Always look for how to make things easier and more obvious, and make the space reflect you and your style. After some time, look for the "logjams" of piled up clutter and go through asking yourself questions about them again.

The best example of this revisiting and tweaking process is a story I tell about a hamper. A family bought a beautiful, expensive wicker hamper for their children's bathroom. Every few days the top of the hamper would be piled high with clothing, with additional shirts and socks on the floor around it. What do you think was the problem with this clutter logjam? It was having a lid on the hamper. We have to create systems that are as easy as possible, and *having a lid* meant that the kids needed two hands to open and shut the hamper and put their clothing inside. Once they removed the lid and left it off, the problem was solved. Now it's a one-handed pretend basketball shot instead of a complicated process.

You may find roadblocks like this one that are simple to solve, or you may have to deal with behavioral issues around maintaining the space. Ask others for their perspectives on the problem, including our team of experts on our member message boards.

STOP and read this before getting a self-storage unit!

Did you know that, as of 2007, seven square feet of commercial storage space existed for every single American? Self-storage facilities are sprouting up around the country like mushrooms. Now that I have pointed this out, you will notice more of them as you drive around. ***What IS all of that stuff?*** These units contain mostly "D" items that are languishing away in their own climate-controlled mausoleums. These facilities often have auctions in which they just sell off the contents of abandoned units.

Before you put anything into a self-storage unit, do the math. ***At some point, the rental cost exceeds the replacement costs of the items inside!*** Is it worth it?

Obviously there are good reasons to utilize these units during times of transition, such as a death, divorce or move. But pause and think carefully before you create your own personal annex of belongings you will never visit.

Clutter Fitness Exercises

- Create a SpaceScaping worksheet for your top priority project.
- Commit to a time with your Motivation Partner when you will have started the project, with a landmark of where you'd like to be next time you talk.

How to Get Organized to Do Organizing

As you jump into your projects, you'll want to make it as easy as possible to get started. Obstacles like gathering up supplies can take up time that you would rather spend organizing. It's best to keep a toolkit together, ideally in a handy cleaning caddy if you can. Here are the tools of the trade:

Your Organizing Toolkit

❑ **Heavy-duty trash bags, lawn and leaf size**

Organizing tends to generate heavy duty trash, and you will need heavy-duty bags. Anything less than 1.1 mil of thickness, which you can read on the package's fine print, will lead to heartache and mess. I personally prefer drawstring closure ties as well.

❑ **Trash can**

To hold trash bags open, we use the "Rubbermaid spring bag" (27 gallon size), originally designed for raking leaves and gardening work, which collapses into a flat hoop when not being used. Every time we use this in our work with clients, they ask, "Where did you get that?" There are other products like this, but we have found this particular model is the only one that actually fits a normal black lawn and leaf bag inside it properly. These are available on Amazon.com or at any Ace Hardware store, where they can order them if they don't have them in stock.

If you don't have the spring bag, use one of your own trash receptacles, but make sure it's large enough to handle a lot of trash. Otherwise it will get full too quickly, and you will get frustrated.

❑ **Label maker**

Of course, being Professional Organizers, we get really excited about label makers. I bought my first one when I was ten, remember? I like the two major brands, Brother and Dymo. I have used a Brother handheld unit for my entire career as a professional, and I have never needed anything more than this compact size. (In 2008, I was honored to represent the truly terrific Brother P-Touch model 1280 as a spokesperson.) For everyday use, I do not recommend buying the larger and heavier desktop units.

❑ **Paper grocery bags and/or boxes for sorting**

Even if you prefer reusable cloth bags, for a little while you can answer "paper" at the grocery store when they ask you the "paper or plastic" question. This will allow you to gather a small collection of paper sacks for use in sorting things. They are perfect for sorting because you can write on them, they stand up on their own, they are pretty tough, and you can just give them away if they are filled with donation items. Boxes are also good, but they are bulkier to store.

❑ **"Elsewhere" Box**

Use one of your paper bags or boxes for this purpose.

❑ **Permanent markers**

We prefer Sharpie® Retractables.

❏ **Timer**

Use a timer to remind you if you want to stop working at a certain time, and timers are also great tools for overcoming procrastination. Bargain with yourself to do something for only ten or 15 minutes. Once you get started, you may even want to continue for a longer time.

❏ **Measuring tape**

A large measuring tape is great for so many reasons. Measure shelves and other items before you go shopping for containers. You also might need to measure furniture before deciding to move it. We recommend having a small three-foot measuring tape in your purse or on your keychain for use while shopping. I love having one of these keychain tapes so much that we had some of our own made to sell in our online store.

❏ **Scissors or a box knife**

You'll need something sharp for cutting open packages, removing price tags, and opening boxes.

❏ **Paper & pen for notes**

A paper and pen are probably the most essential supplies. During a project you will always think of action items to write down, and you'll probably have a shopping list going of things you need to buy to complete your work. Jot down the measurements for certain shelves, items, or cabinet spaces before buying some of the things on your list. And you may have other random thoughts that come up while you are working, so use the paper and pen to capture these thoughts so you won't get sidetracked.

❏ **Water or other beverage**

Go ahead and get something to drink so you won't get distracted by that later. Preferably use a container with a cap on it, so it won't spill on things amid the clutter.

❏ **Phone(s)**

Grab your cordless phone and/or your cellular phone so that you don't
have to scramble when they ring! Alternatively, you can just turn them off
to avoid the distraction. If you do answer the phone, make sure you don't
get sidetracked with your conversation. You may be able to keep sorting
while you talk, depending upon the type of call.

Optional Additions:

- Goo-Gone, for removing stickers
- Museum Putty, for securing items on shelves and keeping drawer
  dividers from sliding
- Sticky notes, various sizes
- Tool belt, to keep your supplies and tools close at hand, save steps,
  and prevent loss
- Furniture marking pens, for touching up furniture scratches
- Cable ties, for cinching up cords and cables
- Paper towels/cleaning rags

Museum Putty, a 3-ft. measuring tape, and a timer are all available in
our online store for your convenience.

Setting the Stage

You're about to start your first project, so don't make the most common
mistake...going "hog-wild" in the Container Store anticipating everything
you're going to need. Get into the project, see what you have remaining
to store, do your measuring, make a list, and only then go out to buy
your supplies. The Container Store is definitely fun, but if the items don't
work, you've created another errand for yourself later when they need to
be returned.

Get your toolkit ready, use the timer to pace yourself in a way that makes you comfortable and energized, and make sure to take breaks during your work to rest and celebrate your progress.

You may need to set up a "staging area" to review and sort, as the space may be too crowded. If you're working on a garage, the driveway is a perfect staging area. If you are working in a bedroom, you might need to create your groups and piles of items in the hallway or another bedroom.

Establish a "Supply Spot" where you locate all of the potential organizing supplies that you find and purchase. When we do a large project like a move, we always make a Supply Spot somewhere downstairs in the home where we can pick and choose from the sorters and bins and baskets we've found as we work. It's like having our own little store.

Where Do I Start?

If you're still not sure which project to do first, here is some additional guidance. As a general rule, it's wisest to start in the most immediately beneficial areas, like your daily living areas needed to perform basic functions such as cooking, sleeping, washing and relaxing. Work on creating these systems first to support you with all the new things that will continually flow into your life as the process continues. Then, work into your "C" and "D" storage areas at home.

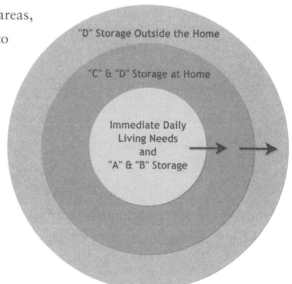

If you have outside storage units or other secondary storage that needs to be addressed, unless the expense and stress of that is really weighing on you, it's better to address your primary living areas first so you'll not be tempted to bring additional things into that space and "mess up the good work" that you've already done.

Our diagram here shows working from the inside of the circle, your immediate daily living needs, outward to the lesser used areas of the home and beyond.

Ready, Set, Go!

Now that you're completely prepared with the O.R.D.E.R. approach, your plan, and your toolkit, use our *Room by Room Recipes* section in the back of this book to get the particular advice for the space you're organizing.

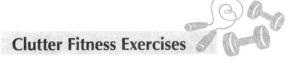

Clutter Fitness Exercises

- Get your Organizing Toolkit put together. If you don't have all of the supplies, it's okay. At least have some good trash bags, a measuring tape, the paper bags, and a pen and paper. That will get you started.

- Check the *Room by Room Recipes* section and read up on the project you'd like to do first.

- Take some "before" photos. Don't forget! Having these photos is extremely motivating later when you see how far you've come. You can also submit your photos for our program's Success Stories contest and win!

- Get started on your project and let your Motivation Partner know how it's going. If you're a paid member of our program, tell us about what you're doing on the message boards. We'd love to see your photos and help you!

Maintenance

The Foundation of Home Organization: Systems & Routines

In my experience and analysis of this subject over many years, I have identified three different types of organizing:

1. Planning

2. Projects and

3. Systems & Routines.

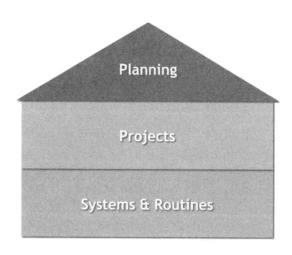

Planning is the highest level of organizing and the least often done. Doing your Clutter Fitness Workbook exercises is a great example of planning, as well as weekly planning of menus or calendars and making vacation arrangements. Planning is the time that you take to step back and think ahead, whether it's daily, weekly or long-term.

Projects pertain to a specific area, like a closet or a garage, when you focus only on that particular space and get it done. Projects are usually the reason people call us for services in person. Many of the "dishes" on our program's weekly menu plans are projects, both large and small. One of the big mistakes many people make in their organizing endeavors is having a tendency to focus too much on Projects and not enough on the other two types.

Systems and Routines are located at the bottom of our little house diagram, because they are really the *foundation* of home organization. All of us have routine tasks we need to perform on a daily basis, both morning and evening, to keep our homes functioning on the most basic levels of eating, sleeping, dressing and living. Weekly tasks have to be done to keep things clean and maintained, and there are also monthly and seasonal needs in most homes, like bathing the dog or changing air filters. *These systems and routines are essential to keeping a household properly organized.*

These three types of organizing each support one another and overlap. You may do some Planning in order to approach a Project, you may do some Planning as part of a regular Routine, and, in all likelihood, you have a Routine to help you maintain a Project you completed. In this section of the book you will be doing some Planning to make sure these Systems and Routines get accomplished regularly.

The following components are vital to successful Systems & Routines:

- **Infrastructure:** Having the right equipment and locations set up to accomplish the tasks. Your organizing projects, as discussed in previous chapters, help you create this infrastructure by identifying and customizing the functions and flow of the spaces.

- **Ownership:** Knowing to whom the tasks belong. I can't tell you how many times I have experienced this myself: "I thought *you* were going to do that!" "No, I thought you were supposed to do it." When there isn't clarity on ownership, everyone thinks someone else is going to do it and the task simply doesn't get done.

- **Commitment:** Agreement and understanding that these tasks need to get done and why. If you are performing the tasks, you commit to them and put them on your schedule. If you are delegating tasks to others, get a commitment from them, explain the consequences of not doing the tasks, and help them create a way to remind themselves.

- **Execution:** Actually doing the tasks (or accepting the consequences of not doing them).

You may have been doing it all yourself...that is a common situation. Many times we (especially women) don't stop our busy lives to think about how we could delegate certain components of the systems. Children, for example, can do many things if some thought is given to exactly which tasks are appropriate, such as setting the table, folding towels or helping with pet care. Sometimes spouses are simply unaware of how they can help and are happy to do so when given clear instructions and *ownership*.

This section of the book will help you make decisions about the tasks you want to do, how often you want to do them, and the ownership of them so that you can then communicate the plan to your family or housemates and gain their commitment. The fact that you are the person going through this exercise means that you will probably have ownership of the whole plan.

You may need to oversee the execution of tasks and follow through on consequences if they're not done. Ideally, if you can get others to go through this planning process with you, you will gain stronger commitment and more ideas of how the process could work better.

The next chapter helps you formulate your morning and evening routines—the tasks you need to attend to daily to make sure your life runs smoothly.

The following chapters cover the four basic systems essential for any home and help you make a plan for your own customized structure for each.

The four basic systems are below, with a few examples of the tasks that comprise them:

Administration
- Family and personal activities
- Purchasing and errands
- Financial and administrative tasks

Cleaning
- Laundry
- Vacuuming/Sweeping/Mopping
- Dusting
- Straightening
- Everything else it takes to keep your home sanitary and healthy

Maintenance
- Lawn care
- Care of possessions like cars
- Repairs
- Organizing projects and appliances

Meals
- Meal planning
- Cooking
- Dishes

Adding New Habits to Your Life

The systems and routines you develop may require you to add new habits to your life, and those are behavioral changes with which you might need help to achieve. Utilize the support of your Motivation Partner for making these changes, remembering that the odds of completing your goals increase with additional accountability! Here are the probabilities again:

According to the American Society of Training and Development, the probability of completing a goal is:

10% if you hear an idea

25% if you consciously decide to adopt it

40% if you decide when you will do it

50% if you plan how you will do it

65% if you commit to someone else you will do it

95% if you have a specific accountability appointment with the person to whom you committed

Going through these planning exercises means that *you're already halfway there!*

Adding too many new habits at once can be a recipe for failure and a perfect set-up for "All or Nothing Thinking." I once knew a sedentary meat-eater and smoker who decided to quit smoking, take up an exercise program, and become a vegetarian all at once. I am sure you can guess how that turned out! It was full speed ahead, and then at the first "failure," the attempts were seen as completely futile and all was lost. Let's explore how we can add new habits and make changes on a slower, more realistic basis.

You may have seen Martha Beck on the Oprah Winfrey show. She is a life coach and speaker, and one of her books is called *The Four-Day Win*, a weight-loss book. Her book is a masterful explanation of motivation, in which she explains how to break big goals into smaller ones and incorporate them into your life in a manageable way.

She discusses the somewhat magical quality of doing something four times. If you have gone snowboarding, for example, one time, you will say that you did that once. If you've done it two times, you'll say you've done it twice. If you've gone three times, you will tell people you've done it a few times. But if you've gone snowboarding four times, something switches, and you finally say, "I snowboard." *I do that.*

Beck suggests that you create a daily goal—maybe it's doing the morning routine tasks we're about to discuss. She advises that you keep cutting that goal in half until it's "ridiculously attainable." For example, maybe doing a big morning routine is too much to add to your life all at once. You can start with just the goal of emptying the dishwasher, which is definitely achievable.

Next, she recommends doing this task daily for four days and setting a small daily reward for achieving that. So when you have put away the dishes in the mornings, you'll allow yourself a treat of watching one of your favorite shows that evening, or maybe you let yourself linger over your favorite blogs.

Finally, you set a larger reward for the end of the four days upon completing all four daily goals. Perhaps in this scenario you buy yourself some new kitchen towels or go to a movie. The idea is that now you have started a habit of putting away the clean dishes each morning.

> That which we persist in doing becomes easier, not that the task itself has become easier, but that our ability to perform it has improved.
> - Ralph Waldo Emerson

You can continue to add more habits to your life in just the same way. You can also try what we call "Habit Hooks," in which you anchor a new habit onto an already established one. The best example is flossing when you are brushing your teeth. You already brush, so you remember to floss because you've anchored those activities together. Here are some other Habit Hooks:

While you are already doing this...	You can add this habit on...
Pumping gasoline	Clean out your car. There is plenty of time to do this while you wait, and there is a trash can already there at the pump.
Taking the garbage out on trash day	Clean out your refrigerator. Doing this at the right time prevents smells from building up from spoiled food.
Paying bills	Clean out your purse. You may need some of the receipts in your purse while you are working on this task.
Celebrating your birthday	Give yourself the gift of health by scheduling your annual physical exam.
Driving together as a family to a weekly meeting or worship service	Take your calendars along in the car and have a weekly planning session with your spouse. Decide which person is responsible that week for dinners, errands, driving children and other shared tasks, and make sure you have a sitter or other needs discussed and resolved.
Making breakfast	Take the laundry to its next step. Move clothes from the washer to the dryer or fold a finished load while you wait for eggs to boil or toast to cook.
Celebrating St. Patrick's Day and Labor Day; or Easter and Halloween; or Memorial Day and Thanksgiving	Change your tap water filters. Many filters need to be changed twice a year, so hook this habit on to your favorite holidays that are six months apart.

Clutter Fitness Exercises

- Raise your right hand up high. Bend your elbow so your right hand touches your left shoulder. Now, *pat yourself on the back*, because you are in Planning mode! Just going through this book and doing your Clutter Fitness Exercises means you are halfway there!

Creating Your Morning and Evening Routines

Morning and evening times are often "crunch time" for busy families. There are deadlines like bedtimes and school buses and many things to accomplish. Some of these tasks are tricky and met with great resistance, like baths and homework! We get caught up in our lives, without a plan, and we forget that a few simple rules and a few tasks done at the right time could make everything run much more smoothly.

Think of yourself as your own best friend. How can your routines help your Future Self tomorrow? What would make him or her smile? What would make him or her feel relieved? Personally, I love that I completely clean up the kitchen in the evening, because my Future Self walks in the next morning to make my cup of tea in a lovely kitchen without anything in the way. Remember that what we do now supports ourselves later!

Morning Routines

Let's look at some of the more common tasks that need to be accomplished in the mornings and see how we can support ourselves to have a smoother day.

- Getting dressed
- Deciding what to eat
- Cleaning/putting away dishes
- Making and eating breakfast
- Starting the laundry
- Feeding and caring for pets
- Exercising
- Getting children to school
- Commuting to work

Our Basic Recommendation: Just D.E.W. it!

We believe that for most families, the "Morning To-D.E.W. List" is the best way to start every day. Meals and laundry are the hardest systems to maintain consistently when you are tired at the end of the day. If your needs are different, you can develop your own morning routine based on what is important to you. Your Clutter Fitness Workbook will provide space to write down your personal morning routine.

Dishes: Is the dishwasher ready for receiving new dishes today? Empty the clean dishes from the dishwasher that you ran the night before.

Eating: What are you going to eat today? Do you need to thaw something or prepare something in advance? Maybe you only make reservations, but make a decision.

Wash: What is the status of the laundry? Can you move it to the next stage?

You may need to get up earlier to do some of these things at first. Remember that adding too many new habits all at once can set you up for failure! Don't expect to perform miracles all at once. Add in one thing at a time and see how it goes, and be kind! Watch out for defeatist language that communicates negative and permanent messages, like "I'll never get this right."

What we do in the morning supports us in the evening. If you've emptied the dishwasher and put away the clean dishes, your kitchen is ready for the lunch, snack and dinner dishes that will collect throughout the day. If you've decided what is for dinner, you are a big step ahead when you get home in the evening and need to cook.

Evening Routines

Let's look now at what typically happens in the evenings in many families' homes:

- Making and eating dinner
- Cleaning dishes/Running the dishwasher
- Moving the laundry forward
- Bathing children
- Helping children with homework
- Feeding and caring for pets
- Making lunches for tomorrow
- Straightening up the house
- Getting ready for the next day
- Securing the house before bed

Our Basic Recommendation:

Do your "SSS's" before catching your ZZZ's!

We believe that for most families, this basic "Triple S" checklist is the best way to end your day to be prepared for tomorrow. What we do in the evening supports us in the morning. If you start the dishwasher, the dishes are ready to put away in the morning when you do your To D.E.W. list. And if you set up everything you need for the morning, you won't be rushing around to do that before the school bus arrives or the carpool leaves.

Straighten up: Do "clutter patrol," picking up and putting away things that are on floors and flat surfaces.

Start the dishwasher: Doing this means dishes are clean in the morning and ready to put away.

Set for tomorrow: What do you need to remember to do each evening that would support you for the next day? Plan ahead for the morning to make sure you are prepared for the next day. You can choose clothing, make lunches and get things grouped together to walk out the door.

Get Your Greens

In some states like California, government offices ask residents to run large appliances at night so that the power grid isn't overloaded during the middle of the day. So doing your Triple S evening routine is an environmentally responsible decision as well!

Clutter Fitness Exercises

- Make your personal morning and evening routine checklists in your workbook, customizing them for your family's needs from the suggested lists. Post your routine summaries where you'll see them and be able to follow them daily. (If for some reason you don't already have your Clutter Fitness Workbook by now, you can download and print it from here: www.clutterdiet.com/book. Registration of your personal information is not required to download this workbook.)

- Add these habits into your day in a realistic and comfortable way that works for you, whether with a "Four Day Win" approach or a "Habit Hook."

- Tell your Motivation Partner your plan to add new habits to your routine, and check in with him or her as you implement this plan.

Consider the

postage stamp;

its usefulness

consists in the ability

to stick to one thing

until it gets there.

– **Josh Billings**

Creating Your Administration System

Have you ever stopped to think about all the roles that are involved in keeping a home? Here are a few of the "hats" that are worn in the role of Administrator of the household:

- Purchasing agent
- Personal shopper
- Chauffeur
- Personal assistant
- Event planner
- Travel agent
- Bookkeeper

- File clerk
- Fleet manager
- IT administrator
- Mail clerk
- Social director
- Archivist

And that list covers only one of the four basic systems of the home! It's a good idea to manage these roles carefully so nothing falls through the cracks.

Your Administration system covers Family and Personal Activities, Event Planning, Purchasing, Errands, Financial Tasks and Other Administrative Tasks. **First read through each of these system descriptions, and at the end of the chapter you'll create your own systems in your Clutter Fitness Workbook.**

Family and Personal Activities

Let's face it, families are busy. Getting a visual representation of a typical week in your family can be helpful in terms of seeing exactly where your time is going and helping you plan better. You can block out your family's regular schedule of these activities on the Weekly Overview Chart, a chart found in your Clutter Fitness Workbook.

You might want to have one version for summer and one for the school year, or even versions for various sports seasons. Some families may need to make a different version for each busy family member. Going through this exercise will help you fit in the things that are missing (like exercise and relaxation time, usually). Here is a memory jogging list of activities to help you recall as many as you can:

- Work and school
- Sports practices and games
- Music and other lessons
- Clubs and associations
- Community involvement
- Pet care and feeding

- Exercise classes
- Play dates and social engagements
- Family fun—movies, etc.
- Religious activities or classes
- Medical appointments

To manage all of these activities, we highly recommend doing "Sunday Planning." Sunday Planning is a time for families to convene about the week ahead. It doesn't have to be on Sunday if that doesn't work for you, but typically Sunday evenings are not as heavily scheduled as other nights, and it comes before the beginning of the new work and school week.

You don't have to call a formal family meeting unless you want to do so. If you have a weekly drive to a religious service or other regular activity, that can be the perfect time to do your planning with everyone in the car together. Take just ten minutes to go over these items once a week:

❏ Review your calendar for everyone involved, also using the Weekly Overview Chart if desired
❏ Who is taking whom where, and when?
❏ What evenings might one or both parents need to be out?
❏ Is there a sitter required later in the week?
❏ Who is in charge of homework help?
❏ Who is cooking and doing dishes?
❏ Who is doing bath and bedtime duty for younger children?
❏ Who is cleaning and taking care of other chores?

To make sure these activities and the decisions you make about them are known to all, create a Communication Station. This station should be in a common area, possibly in the kitchen or near where you enter and exit the house. Details about creating a Communication Station are in the *Room by Room Recipes* section near the end of the book.

Event Planning

What events does your family normally celebrate or plan for? Typical households have between 15 and 20 celebrations or events they need to plan for in one year! Get ahead of the curve on these by thinking through what you'll be doing and when. **Here are some memory-jogging suggestions to help you with the Clutter Fitness Exercise at the end of this chapter:**

- New Year's Day
- Sports watching parties
- Valentines' Day
- Spring Break vacations
- Religious holidays and celebrations
- Birthday parties and anniversaries
- Graduation and retirement parties
- Father's and Mother's Day
- Summer camps
- Summer vacations
- Baby showers
- Weddings
- Fourth of July celebrations
- Labor Day picnics
- Halloween
- Thanksgiving
- Winter cultural holidays (Christmas, Hanukkah, Kwanzaa)
- Other occasions unique to your family traditions

Purchasing

What happens when you run out of an item or otherwise realize that you need to buy something? You need to have an accepted place where everyone writes things down to be purchased. This shopping list should be paper, not a wipe-off board or chalkboard, because you will probably need to take it with you to the store.

The simplest solution is a small, narrow pad of paper that you can buy at almost any office supply store or discount store. You've seen them—cute ones, lined ones, ones with funny sayings on them. Whatever you like, just use it! You can even use scratch paper from around your house, as long as it has an identified, consistent home (like the refrigerator or pantry door), there is a writing utensil next to it at all times, and everyone knows the purpose of the paper.

The better solution is to have a preprinted list of commonly-used items, because it's easy to circle what you need, and it also reminds you of things you might have forgotten. If you collect your used lists for a month or so, you can easily create your own on your computer and print it on scratch paper. (You can also buy a preprinted shopping list pad with a magnet on it in our online store.)

You might want to organize items on the list first by the store, then roughly by the section or aisle, like, "Produce," "Deli," "Dairy" and others. You also might want to have multiple lists if you often shop at various stores. In my family, for example, we shop at a grocery store, a warehouse store and a discount store.

You can purchase pens with a chain or coiled tether at any office supply store, just like the banks use, so you'll always have a pen near your list. They stick with adhesive to most surfaces. I recommend purchasing a few refills for these pens at the same time you buy them initially, so that it won't be difficult to find them later.

One of our clients actually took her shopping list one step further. She made a photocopy of the package of each item she frequently purchased and laminated it. She then sorted the laminated cards as she found the need to buy something. In this case, either her housekeeper or spouse would often do the shopping and take the cards along, and with this system they did not purchase the wrong flavor, variety or size! Her system was probably a little over-engineered, but it's an example of how you can get creative.

If you have a computer in or near your kitchen, you can try using the free software from Cozi.com, which (along with a family calendar) features multiple shopping lists that can be sent via text message to you on demand. Imagine stopping by the grocery store and sending a text message to get your list sent to you on the spot! If you are technically-inclined, you might enjoy experimenting with this option.

If your family likes to clip and use coupons, incorporate this practice into your purchasing system. Most coupon experts recommend using an accordion file or a binder with page protectors and sleeves to sort them by category. *Suggested categories:* Auto Services, Clothing, Electronics, Entertainment, Frequent Buyer Cards, Gift Certificates, Groceries, Household, Lawn & Garden, Other, Personal Services, Pets and Restaurants.

Obviously, if you are a prolific coupon clipper, you will want to subdivide the category of "Groceries" much further. You can learn quite a bit about the art of couponing, which I daresay has its own "subculture" of frugal fans. Good online resources include CouponMom.com and Mommysavers.com.

Errands

Closely related to organizing your purchasing is errands, those little trips we regularly take around town that keep our household running smoothly. We recommend that you try to consolidate your errands to one day per week whenever possible. Doing this enables you to plan your route for efficiency, saving time and gas. Some people like keeping last year's Yellow Pages in the back of their vehicle for reference and planning when running errands. Keeping a collapsible-style cooler or cooler bag in your vehicle can help you consolidate your errands more efficiently without worrying about melting or spoiling groceries.

While you're out, you may need information to get around better. Your cellular phone service probably offers directions, restaurant reservations, movie times and other assistance through their 411 information line. This service usually costs a small fee per call but can make all the difference in saving time and hassle. Also, readers who live in the United States can send a text message to Google at 466453 ("GOOGLE") and get an enormous amount of information such as addresses and directions for free (your standard text message rates do apply). A typical message you might send for address and phone information would use a keyword or specific store name, plus your zip code or city, such as "hardware store Austin," "sushi 90210," or "Starbucks 10019." Read more about how to use this free service at www.google.com/sms.

If you have a lot of purchases to make, during a move, perhaps, or when building a new house, keep a small Shopping Notebook in your car. Include a map of your local mall, so if you need to go to one store, you'll know what entrance will save you the most steps. Also in the notebook, keep swatches of your wallpaper, measurements and pictures of your furniture, paint colors and fabrics for matching items to your home decor.

Try to avoid errands in the first place by doing as much as possible online. You can literally get almost anything you need from the Internet! You may recall a man named Mitch Maddox who, in 2000, legally changed his name to "DotComGuy" and vowed to live in his Dallas home for one full year without ever leaving. He successfully ordered everything he needed online and had it delivered. Think about how much time, gas and wear and tear on his car that he saved!

Financial and Other Administrative Tasks

As much as we like to think that "all we need is love," we really do need money to make a household stay functional. Who takes care of this in your home? Someone must pay the bills, and someone also has to check the mail, fill out forms, file insurance claims, call the pest control service, file papers, fix computers and otherwise keep things afloat.

While reviewing the list that follows, think about who has ownership of these financial and other administrative tasks in your home. Try to delegate some of these items if you are the one doing it all!

- Checking mail
- Sorting and distributing mail
- Maintaining the filing system
- Paying bills
- Reconciling statements
- Preparing tax returns
- Managing vendors and services
- Cleaning off bulletin board and/or children's artwork
- Maintaining address book or contact database
- Managing photos and memorabilia
- Making miscellaneous calls and completing forms
- Running computer backups and other IT maintenance
- Filing insurance claims
- Registering vehicles and having cars inspected

What Kids Can Do:

- Gather relevant papers from backpacks and school bags to give to parents.
- Put things on the family calendar and the shopping list if they are old enough to write.
- Communicate errands they need to have done for them.
- Help directly by running errands (if they are old enough to drive).
- Check and sort the mail.
- File reference papers into an established filing system.
- Enter addresses into a contact database.

Clutter Fitness Exercises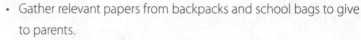

Family and Personal Activities:

- Outline a Weekly Overview Chart for your family's activities in your Clutter Fitness Workbook.

- What changes will you make in your family for planning, scheduling, and communicating?

Event Planning:

- Use the planning tool in your workbook to decide when you need to plan for these celebrations. For each occasion, write down the date it occurs and the date you need to start planning for it, along with whom you can ask for help. When you're finished, put the advance planning date on your calendar, or Clutter Diet members can use our e-mail reminder system to prompt you when it's time.

- Clutter Diet members can find our Entertaining Checklist in our Knowledge Base for help planning any of these individual events.

Purchasing:

- What changes will you make to streamline the purchasing in your home?

Errands:

- Is there a person in the neighborhood with whom you could consolidate errands?

- Is there a young driver in your home or neighborhood who would enjoy making some extra money helping you? Write down ideas you have about whom this might be and contact him or her.

- Are there errands you have been neglecting, like car washing and maintenance, that need to be scheduled and done? Schedule a time to do them or delegate them.

- What changes will you make to get errands down to a minimum of time and expense?

Financial and Other Administrative Tasks:

- Complete the planning tool in your workbook, assigning ownership and frequency to these tasks. Add relevant scheduling to your calendar or your Clutter Diet e-mail reminders. Discuss the ownership of these tasks and gain commitment with anyone to whom you have delegated. If possible, incorporate some of the processes into your Weekly Overview Chart in the workbook.

Creating Your Cleaning System

One of the "occupational hazards" of my profession is that people often think I am an expert on cleaning things. I am definitely not an expert on getting stains out of clothing or knowing 101 household uses for vinegar, but I do like talking about organizing your systems and schedules to get the cleaning done.

The good news: There are many ways to clean a house, mostly depending upon your preferences and definitions of what "clean" really means. Everyone's home, family, and situation is different, so I cannot tell you exactly when you need to mop your floors and wash your bath mats. You may not even have bath mats, so I have created a framework to help you make a plan for your own household.

As in the previous chapter, read through this information first, then make your plan in your Clutter Fitness Workbook in the exercises at the end.

Laundry

Our Laundry Cycle diagram illustrates the never-ending process of laundry in the typical household. You may not have thought through this system entirely before. There are quite a few steps!

Consider these steps and think about how to divide up your family's laundry duties in a more equitable and pleasing way. Discuss with your family members which steps they like and which steps they don't enjoy about laundry (no fair to say you don't like any of them!). In my home, for example, I really don't mind gathering, sorting, washing and drying, but I don't like folding and putting away. So we divide it up that way between my husband and me, and my children do their own laundry on the weekends (with shepherding and coordination on our part).

Wearing clothes

Putting clothes away in rooms

Putting dirty clothes in hamper

Ironing or repairing if needed

Gathering of dirty clothing

The Laundry Cycle

Folding or hanging dry clothes

Sorting of dirty clothing

Drying or hanging up to dry

Pretreating stains

Washing clothes

There are several ways of doing laundry in terms of frequency. Some people prefer to do one load daily all the way through, as we recommend as part of your morning routine. Others want to save it all up and do it once a week. And some may want to do everything every other day. For your personal plan, decide on a strategy and really stick to it! We believe if you have children it's best to do it daily, as it piles up quickly and becomes overwhelming.

A timer is a really helpful tool with laundry. Sometimes you would have been easily able to do the next step of the laundry if you had been reminded, and a timer can help, particularly if your machines don't have a signaling feature or you can't hear it in parts of your house. Pay attention to how long your washing and drying cycles take so you'll know how long to set the timer.

If you're experiencing laundry pile-ups anywhere in the process, study our Laundry Cycle diagram and give some thought to which steps are typically causing bottlenecks. Is it an ownership problem (identifying whose responsibility to do it)? Is it an infrastructure problem (not a good place or right equipment to do it)? Or is it an execution problem (not doing it when you're supposed to—like kids leaving clothes on the floor)? Again, put your Sherlock Holmes hat on and be a problem-solver.

Vacuuming, Dusting, Bathrooms and Other Cleaning Tasks

Few people truly love cleaning, so the best advice we can give you is this:

- Keep your systems going consistently—don't let it go too long, or it becomes overwhelming.
- Listen to audiobooks or music to distract you while you work.
- Hire cleaning help if you possibly can, even every other week or monthly. Consider the value of your leisure time!

- Get your kids involved—it teaches them respect for the house.

- Look for shortcuts whenever you can—we like the book *Speed Cleaning* by Jeff Campbell.

- Reward yourself for your cleaning efforts—even a small reward can be satisfying.

- Remember the "have a party" method of creating a deadline for yourself. Preparing for guests will definitely get you in gear!

- Leverage the relationship with your Motivation Partner to support you in getting your cleaning done.

It's important to be realistic when planning the frequency of these tasks. It may sound like a great idea to take all the curtains down and wash them quarterly, but the reality is that you may only get to this once a year at best. Don't set yourself up for disappointment or an "All or Nothing Thinking" trap!

Many homeowners who do their own cleaning do it on the weekend, perhaps on a Saturday, in a large block of time. Weekends are typically the best time if you are going to get the family involved. Make sure your supplies are replenished and you have good mops, sponges and other tools.

Every home is different, so we've provided a list of normal cleaning tasks that are common to most houses. Feel free to add tasks that are unique to your home in your workbook when you do your Clutter Fitness Exercises at the end of the chapter.

Bathrooms:
- Change hand towels, check toilet paper and tissue, clean "the seat"
- Clean toilet, tub, shower, sinks, mirror and counters
- Clean floors

- Wash the bath mats
- Clean light fixtures
- Wash windows and windowsills
- Clean the bathroom scale and trash cans
- Clean and polish cabinets and tiles
- Tackle the heavy cleaning: grout, baseboards, corners, switch plates

Bedrooms:
- Change sheets
- Dust and vacuum
- Clean under bed
- Wash mattress protectors
- Straighten closets and drawers
- Clean light fixtures and/or lamps
- Wash windows and windowsills
- Turn mattresses
- Clean window treatments/blinds
- Check for cobwebs and dust picture frames
- Tackle heavy cleaning: shelves, baseboards, switch plates, doorknobs
- Take comforters to dry cleaner

Entryway and Formal Living and Dining Areas, if applicable:
- Dust and vacuum
- Check for cobwebs and dust picture frames
- Dusting detail: inside china cabinets or other special areas
- Vacuum furniture
- Tackle heavy cleaning: baseboards, corners, switch plates, doorknobs
- Clean light fixtures and/or lamps
- Polish silver if applicable

- Wash windows and windowsills
- Clean fireplaces and vents
- Clean window treatments/blinds

Exterior:
- Sweep porches and sidewalks
- Sweep garage
- Shovel snow if applicable
- Clean patio furniture
- Clean porches with water hose
- Clean grill or outdoor eating area
- Clean windows
- Clean exterior light fixtures

Family Room/Other Living Areas:
- Straighten up toys/video games
- Dust and vacuum
- Check for cobwebs and dust picture frames
- Dusting detail: shelving and entertainment center areas
- Vacuum furniture
- Tackle heavy cleaning: baseboards, corners, switch plates, doorknobs
- Clean light fixtures and/or lamps
- Straighten up bookshelves/ media/music collections
- Wash windows and windowsills
- Clean fireplaces and vents
- Clean window treatments/blinds

Kitchens:

- Change dishtowels and washcloths and/or sanitize sponges
- Wipe down table and all countertops; clean kitchen sink
- Take out trash
- Clean floors
- Clean highchairs or other baby-related gear
- Clean out refrigerator of spoiled food and wipe down shelves
- Clean microwave
- Deep clean the refrigerator
- Clean oven and stovetop
- Clean throw rugs
- Clean toaster/coffee machine/other small appliances
- Defrost freezer and clean drip pans and coils underneath refrigerator
- Clean/polish cabinet fronts
- Wash trash can
- Tackle heavy cleaning: baseboards, corners, switch plates, doorknobs
- Clean stove exhaust fan
- Clean ice maker
- Wash canisters and knick-knacks
- Clean light fixtures
- Wash windows and windowsills
- Clean window treatments/blinds

Overall and Miscellaneous:

- Take trash bin to curb and return bins after pickup
- "Ladder Day"—cleaning everything up high (shelves, fans, etc.)
- Pet cleanup (bird cages, fish tanks)
- Move furniture when vacuuming

What Kids Can Do:

- Fold laundry—even little ones can fold dishtowels and washcloths.
- Operate laundry machines, starting at about 5 or 6 years old.
- Process at least one load a week all the way through, or even be in charge of doing all of their own laundry when age-appropriate.
- Pretend they are working with you, using safe tools and cleaning supplies. At a young age they can use a rag to dust a table or sweep the floor with a small broom. Children even 3 or 4 years old can do a surprising number of things to clean. Visit a Montessori classroom sometime and be amazed at what the children do there!
- Be responsible for their own rooms as much as possible for their ages.

Clutter Fitness Exercises

Complete the planning tools for laundry and other cleaning tasks in your Clutter Fitness Workbook, assigning ownership and frequency to the steps and tasks. Add relevant scheduling to your calendar or your Clutter Diet e-mail reminders. Discuss the ownership of these tasks and gain commitment with anyone to whom you have delegated. If possible, incorporate some of the process into your Weekly Overview Chart.

Creating Your Maintenance System

We brush our teeth every day, twice a day, because it would be ridiculous to save all of our tooth brushing up for one day out of the month, do it 60 times, and expect the same result. Similarly, you would not expect to do one colossal annual lawn-mowing.

Doing a little easy work each day makes much more sense than doing a bunch of hard work later, all at once. Maintenance routines for our homes help us distribute our tasks over time and do the easy work instead of the hard.

Organizing Projects

As we discussed doing organizing projects earlier in the book with our O.R.D.E.R. acronym, maintaining the projects you completed is part of the process. Like the colossal annual lawn-mowing example, wouldn't it make sense for you to organize a little of your closet throughout the year, keeping it up over time, rather than doing giant organizing projects every year or two?

Being a paid member of the Clutter Diet program means that you will be prompted at the right times to maintain your garage, pantry or sock drawer. We have designed our weekly plans comprehensively to make sure we covered all areas of your house over time. We created it for the average North American family, with seasonal celebrations and climate taken into consideration. So you can just "weigh in" each week and get your house in shape!

If you're not planning on being a member of our program, you can create a system from our workbook and remind yourself using your calendar and checklists. You might also be interested in the book *Sidetracked Home Executives*, by Pam Young and Peggy Jones, which promotes the use of a 3" x 5" card system as a tickler file to maintain your home. Here are the basic instructions for the "S.H.E." system:

1. You'll need a set of lined 3" x 5" index cards and a larger-than-normal index card file box, found at office supply stores. They are similar in size to a shoebox and have a sliding brace to hold up the cards at the back. Tape a small year-at-a-glance calendar to your box lid as a reference, so you can quickly see which days correspond to which dates during the month.

2. Create a card for each job and indicate the frequency on it, such as Daily, Weekly, Monthly or Annually. You can also indicate Quarterly or "2x/Yr" for twice a year. An example might be "Wash Bath Mats—Weekly." You can use different colors of 3" x 5" index cards if you'd like to categorize them or indicate ownership of the jobs using the colors. After writing the title, use the rest of the card for instructions or notes indicating the last time the job was done.

3. File each job card within the 1-31 dividers (representing the days of the current month) and January-December card dividers, according to when the job needs to be done next. (Use your

Hard work is often the easy work you did not do at the proper time.

-Bernard Metzler

Weekly Overview Chart from our Clutter Fitness Workbook to help you decide what to do when, based on your family's activities and which days you would typically clean, run errands, or do administrative tasks.)

4. Check the box daily and complete the cards for that day, then file them away at the next appropriate date for the frequency it requires. If you like, you can rotate the numbered divider for that day to the back of the row upon completion, so that "today" is always showing in the front.

5. On the 25th of the month, put in a card that indicates you should check next month's cards in the January-December dividers, and file those into your 1-31 dividers to do in the coming month.

This tickler file system works really well! The key is checking the box daily and continuing to rotate the cards through the process. Many people have successfully applied this system over the years from Pam and Peggy's popular book. You can use it to remind yourself of just about anything related to any of our systems in this section, from lawn care to birthdays.

Clutter Diet members can also use our customized e-mail reminder system to implement some of these same ideas. Our members can set up recurring e-mail reminders in any increment, such as daily, every 3 days, every 2 months, every year or any other frequency. You can set up a reminder to give the dog his monthly medication, and each month our system will send you an e-mail message at the right time to prompt you.

Landscaping and Lawn Care

Like cleaning, landscaping needs will be varied and unique to each home and even climate. New Mexico residents may have a yard full of decorative gravel instead of grass, for example. Here we have provided you with a list of general guidelines that can be customized in your workbook:

- Watering plants and lawn
- Mowing and edging and weed-trimming
- Mulching and weeding the flowerbeds
- Fertilizing the lawn and the flowerbeds
- Trimming the shrubs
- Spreading bait—"Fire Ant Patrol"
- Potting plants and annual florals
- Trimming trees, checking for wayward branches
- Raking or blowing leaves
- Raking gravel

Indoor Maintenance Tasks

These are tasks that need to be done to maintain the function of the interior of your home, prevent problems and reduce wear and tear. You may have many more things to add to this list depending upon your home, the geographic region in which you live and the climate. Note that this list includes safety and security items—make sure you consider your own home's unique safety and security needs as we cannot possibly anticipate all scenarios. You can create your personal plan for handling these tasks in your Clutter Fitness Workbook:

- Water indoor plants
- Change air filters
- Change water filters or softener unit refills
- Check sump pump in basement to verify that it's working
- Lubricate all door hinges and garage door
- Re-caulk all bathrooms

- Seal grout, marble, brick floors, or tile floors
- Clean dryer exhaust vent
- Change code on garage keypad for security purposes periodically
- Test the carbon monoxide detectors
- Inspect and restock first aid kits
- Change batteries on smoke detectors
- Check fire extinguishers
- Do touch-ups on furniture and cover scratches
- Touch-up interior paint
- Change light bulbs
- Check the house for water leaks
- Inspect the water heaters
- Have chimney swept

Outdoor Maintenance Tasks

These are tasks that need to be done to maintain the function of the exterior of your home, prevent problems and reduce wear and tear. Your needs may vary, as we have been saying, so think through your home and add the tasks into your workbook that pertain to your situation. If you live in Florida, for example, you may need to pick up squashed mangoes off the lawn. Note that this list also includes safety and security items—make sure you consider your own home's unique safety and security needs as we cannot possibly anticipate all scenarios.

- Salt porches, steps, and sidewalks for ice
- Check for bees' nests, exterminate, knock down—"Wasp Nest Patrol"
- Touch-up exterior paint
- Power wash driveways and porches
- Clean gutters

- Inspect weather-stripping around doors, replace if needed
- Have roof inspected
- Put freezing protection on outdoor water spigots
- Change bulbs in exterior lighting fixtures
- Install holiday lighting
- Inspect fencing, do repairs and touch-up
- Take vehicles to shop for repairs, inspections and maintenance

What Kids Can Do:
- Help with weeding, pruning, watering and other gardening tasks. Kids love to be outside, especially when their parents are outside with them. Just make sure whatever they are doing is age appropriate and safe!
- Older kids certainly can mow and water the lawn.
- Water indoor plants with a small watering bucket.
- Watch what their parents are doing and join in at whatever level they can participate.

Clutter Fitness Exercises

Complete the planning tools for organizing projects, indoor and outdoor maintenance, and landscaping tasks in your Clutter Fitness Workbook, assigning ownership and frequency to the steps and tasks. Add relevant scheduling to your calendar or your Clutter Diet e-mail reminders. Discuss the ownership of these tasks and gain commitment with anyone to whom you have delegated. If possible, incorporate some of the process into your Weekly Overview Chart.

Creating Your Meals System

It's the dreaded 6:00PM question: **"What's for dinner?"** Almost nothing is more certain than the fact that we are going to want to eat more than once every day, yet we often have not planned for this obvious eventuality.

There are two parts of your Meals system: Cooking and Dishes. Read through this chapter and then go through the workbook exercises to create your personal plan for getting those meals on the table and cleaning them up.

Cooking

You don't have to be a Food Network star to create simple, healthy meals for your family. So often when people have trouble cooking at home, the culprit is really planning, not a lack of know-how or recipes or even ingredients. Most of our clients have decent collections of cookbooks and pantries full of food. I really believe half the battle is the *decision* of what to cook.

In our Administration system chapter, we talked about "Sunday Planning." **Part of your Sunday Planning can be choosing which person will cook which meals.** You can base this on working opposite the Dishes system (whomever cooks, the others will do dishes). You can also decide based on who is most conveniently able to cook at a given time, considering your family's schedules. Rotate and alternate turns for variety, by day or by week.

Along with deciding whom will be cooking, spend a few minutes on Sundays planning when and what to cook. Here are a few ideas to make this task easier, as these decisions are often the obstacle for eating well at home:

- **Consider a "Rotation Menu"**—make a list of 25 of your family's favorite meals and plug them automatically into a calendar. We offer a form for this on our Free Tips page on our website: http://www. clutterdiet.com/freetips Click on "Rotation Menu Form."

- **Choose one or two nights per week that are easy, such as dining out or leftovers,** and decide these based on activities happening that week—consider practices, games and other outings that may require quicker meals.

- **Use a meal preparation service.** There are many of these franchises around the country, and the cost per serving is often less than if you bought the groceries yourself! Go to DreamDinners.com or SuperSuppers.com to find a location near you. These services are fantastic! You can assemble 12 meals for your freezer in one to two hours, which eliminates the steps of planning and purchasing altogether.

- **Get help online from sixoclockscramble.com,** which provides a family-friendly eating plan and shopping list for a nominal fee each month.

Now that you've decided what to cook, make a shopping list immediately based on the plan for the week, and make certain you have all of the required ingredients to avoid repeat trips to the grocery store. See our previous chapter on Administration, where we discuss your Purchasing system.

To execute the plan, make sure your daily routines include preparing for dinner early in the day. Our D.E.W. morning routine (Dishes, Eating, Wash—just D.E.W. it!) means that items that need thawing or marinating will get their due attention at the right time.

Dishes

The beautiful, delicious meal is done, and everyone scatters. Sound familiar? You might need to assign ownership of some of these clean-up components:

- Clearing the table
- Putting away leftover food
- Loading the dishwasher
- Hand-washing
- Drying dishes
- Wiping stove, counters and tables
- Cleaning the sink
- Emptying the dishwasher
- Putting away all clean dishes

If you use our recommended D.E.W. and Triple S routines for morning and evening, the clean dishes get put away in the morning and the dishwasher gets started in the evening.

As mentioned before, you can work opposite the Cooking schedule, so that one person cooks, and the other does dishes, and then you can alternate days or weeks with this opposite schedule. You could also assign one person to do all of the cooking and clean-up for one whole day or evening, then alternate days or weeks.

Yet another approach is for each person to take selected component(s) for a week and rotate them. Our boys have alternated weeks of emptying the dishwasher for several years now, and it is part of their morning routines.

What Kids Can Do:

- Help think of meal ideas in general.
- Plan the menu at least one night per week.
- Make side dishes or salads, or at least wash or chop something.
- Set the table. Teaching kids the etiquette of table setting is an important life lesson.
- Older kids can cook meals! Assign them one night per week to cook.
- Wash dishes—even children as young as three can put their own plates in the dishwasher.

Clutter Fitness Exercises

How will your family improve on cooking and dishes? **Complete the planning tools in your Clutter Fitness Workbook, assigning ownership and frequency to the tasks.** Add relevant scheduling to your calendar or your Clutter Diet e-mail reminders. Discuss the ownership of these tasks and gain commitment with anyone to whom you have delegated. If possible, incorporate some of the process into your Weekly Overview Chart.

Balancing It All

Homeostasis is a medical term that refers to the tendency of the human body to seek and maintain balance, in the way that our temperature is always near 98.6 degrees.

What is your house's "HOME-eostasis?" What is that balanced condition of your home to which you would always like to return?

> **Homeostasis** *n.* [(hoh-mee-oh-stay-sis)] The tendency of the body to seek and maintain a condition of balance or equilibrium within its internal environment, even when faced with external changes. A simple example of homeostasis is the body's ability to maintain an internal temperature around 98.6 degrees Fahrenheit, whatever the temperature outside. [8]

Your house's homeostasis results from preventing clutter, reducing the clutter you have to a manageable and acceptable level, and consistently maintaining your home with systems and routines. It's a state of balance and readiness—the kind of feeling you have when you've just straightened up the house for company to come over for dinner. It's a state of satisfaction, pride, and comfort. **Homeostasis is your definition of success!**

There might be different levels of homeostasis depending upon the formality of your current needs. If you need to be ready for your boss to visit, or a local dignitary, or even a camera crew, that is certainly the highest level of readiness! Being ready for a dinner party with friends is another level and being ready for a relaxed weekend is yet another.

We are not talking about perfection, as we've emphasized. **Homeostasis is a flexible state of balance and readiness that is most comfortable for you and your family and adjusts to transitional times and periods of less or more activity in your lives.** The definition will change as your family and situation change.

Here's what a normal level of homeostasis looks and feels like at my house:

Outside:

- The house looks maintained from the street, with the shrubs trimmed, weeds pulled, and the lawn mowed as needed.
- Front porch, sidewalks and driveway are swept as needed.
- The back porch is swept, kids' belongings are corralled, and the patio furniture is ready to use.

Overall:

- All floors are clean enough, considering the kids and pets we have, and are clear of clutter.

- Cobwebs are kept at bay, and insects are controlled.

- The house is in good repair, with light bulbs changed as needed and broken things fixed.

- Things look and feel clean, with forgiveness for reasonable amounts of dust since the last cleaning.

- All phones are on their chargers or their locations are known.

Entry:

- The benches by our front door are clear, meaning things left there to take upstairs or elsewhere have been put away.

- The stairs are clear of anything needing to be taken upstairs, or if something remains, it will be taken up on the next trip.

Garage and Back Door:

- Our garage is straightened, the floor is swept, and cardboard boxes are broken down next to the trash bins.

- Our back door area has no shoes and other clutter impeding the pathway, and our "Destination Station" shelving is neat and maintained. (See our *Room by Room Recipes* section for creating your own Destination Station.)

Kitchen:

- The kitchen has an empty sink, washed countertops, and an absence of unattended food and dishes. (Okay, maybe a few mugs and glasses are out.)

- Clean dishes are put away.

- Flat surfaces are clear of everything except what is currently being used or is only decorative.

- Homework and other school books and papers are put away or corralled appropriately for current assignments.

- The trash cans have been emptied and the compost has been taken outside.

- The refrigerator is clean and holds only fresh, edible food.
- Appliances are clean and ready to use.
- The pantry holds edible food that is tidy, visible and accessible.

Bathrooms:
- The bathrooms are clean enough to not be embarrassing if a guest were to use them.
- Each bathroom has a decent hand towel, soap, and plenty of toilet paper.

Home Office:
- My office desk is clear of papers and other clutter.
- Shelves are tidy and contain only items that are useful and/or beautiful.
- All unsorted mail has been centralized in my inbox, and ideally, my inbox has been processed and junk mail and reading material have been removed.
- Unfinished tasks and projects have homes and I can find them easily.

Dining Room:
- The dining table is clear of everything except its decorative elements. This often means that we have been folding clothes on the dining table and need to put them away.

Living Room:
- The coffee table holds only recent reading material and is clear of other clutter.
- Pillows are on the sofa and blankets are folded or draped over the sofas.

Utility Room:
- The utility room is free of bottlenecked laundry, meaning clothes are successfully running through the laundry cycle and most of the folded and hanging clothing is put away.

- The top surfaces of the washer and dryer as well as the utility sink are clear of clutter.
- The freezer contains edible food that is visible and accessible.

Bedrooms:

- The closets are tidy but not perfect. Items in closets are visible and accessible.
- Clean clothing is put away and dirty clothing is in hampers.
- Our bed is made and the kids' beds are made... well enough for their ages.
- The kids' rooms are appropriately lived in but tidy enough, with no food or unsanitary conditions.

Playroom (Kids' Lair):

- The playroom is uncluttered, blankets are folded, and pillows are on the sofa.
- Video games and movies are put back where they belong, preferably in their respective cases.
- Remote controls are easily located and have batteries in them.

This list is my homeostasis, my definition of success. It's the level at which I feel most comfortable inviting someone over to visit. Your list will be different, because your home and your family are different. *This is your ultimate goal: To know what homeostasis means for your home and have the education, motivation and support to easily and confidently achieve it when things get out of balance (as they surely will).*

Start Your Own Clutter Diet Today

I hope that the concepts in this book have helped you to see your home as an extension of yourself and a reflection of your life. Getting organized means having your physical environment support you in creating the life you want!

Recall the things that have held you back. And imagine how you now can get beyond them.

Think of the problems that have frustrated you so. And imagine how you can now rise above them.

Look at how far you've come. And imagine how far you can now go.

Think of all that you've learned. And imagine what you can now do with that knowledge.

Consider all you've done in the past year. And imagine what you'll now be able to do.

You're now in a better position than ever to imagine the very best. And what you can imagine will lead to what you can be.

Clutter Fitness Exercises

- What is your definition of success? Paint the picture of "HOME-eostasis" for your own house, using the form in your Clutter Fitness Workbook.

Where Do You Go From Here?

Next steps:

1. Get a Motivation Partner today if you haven't already.

2. Finish doing the exercises in each chapter, utilizing the support and accountability of your Motivation Partner if you are having trouble finishing them.

3. Systems and routines are the foundation of home organization, so they are the highest priority. At the very least, begin with a morning and evening routine and crucial household systems like paying bills. Start small and reward yourself for each improvement.

4. Start tackling your top projects using our *Room by Room Recipes* in the final section of this book.

5. If you wish, join our program online to get personal help and advice and our weekly plan of projects. Our supportive, encouraging member community makes everyone feel welcomed and motivated! And where else can you get direct access to the author of a book you just read, along with a team of other experts, to answer your personal questions for about the price of a pizza? We'd love to see you there.

Set all things in their

own peculiar place,

and know that order

is the greatest grace.

– John Dryden

Room by Room
Recipes

Room by Room Recipes

Administration Station (Home Office)

Ingredients for Success:

We recommend that your home have various "stations" for common functional needs. Seven are featured in this section of the book, the largest being the Administration Station, otherwise known as the home office. Here are the most common functions in this area:

❏ **Calendar**	If at all possible, keep only one master calendar instead of multiple calendars in various places.	
❏ **Task List**	Capture everything in one place so you'll be able to prioritize. If you don't keep this information digitally, use a day planner or a spiral notebook.	
❏ **Contacts**	Centralize all contacts into one system, and delegate the data entry if necessary to make sure the system is updated. Electronic options like Outlook are highly preferable to pen and paper options.	
❏ **E-mail**	Use rules and folders to sort your e-mail automatically as much as possible. Make sure you don't interrupt your day with e-mail processing any more than necessary.	
❏ **Electronic File Structure**	Create a file structure of folders that makes sense for your home and business needs so you (and others sharing the information) can file and find things quickly. Throwing everything into one big "My Documents" folder makes it more difficult to find files. Desktop search software like Google Desktop is also a great solution for electronic files.	
❏ **Data Backups**	Ideally a backup system should be (1) remote, (2) automated, and (3) secure. We like Carbonite.com and Mozy.com.	
❏ **Password Storage**	Don't risk theft of your crucial information by using the same passwords for everything or applying other unsafe practices. Have a secure system for storing these like SplashID software or the Internet Password Organizer books sold on our website at ClutterDiet.com.	
❏ **Software Licenses & CDs**	Software is quite expensive, but many homes and businesses fail to document the license and purchase information that could save them hundreds or thousands in repurchasing costs later. Use a simple spreadsheet to track license numbers and other data for future reference, and print a copy in case your hard drive is damaged.	
❏ **Financial Data**	You may want to use software like Quicken or QuickBooks, and you'll need systems for storing receipts and statements too. Homes and small businesses can often use January-December accordion files to make this simple.	

Types of Paper:

❏ **Quick Reference**	Quick Reference papers are those you need often for handy reference, like frequently called numbers.	
❏ **Reference**	Reference papers simply need to be kept for future reference—no action required.	
❏ **Archives**	An archive system is needed for older reference items.	
❏ **Quick Action**	Quick Action papers require fairly immediate action, like bills to be paid or calls to be made.	
❏ **Projects**	Projects are collections of papers pertaining to multiple steps of actions that have a beginning and end.	

Our Well-Equipped Office diagram has helped many of our clients and members to envision their spaces with these systems in place:

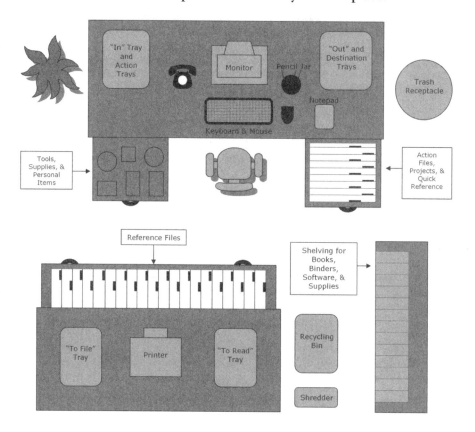

The primary issue most people have in their home offices, and the number one reason people have called us for services in person, is PAPER. So this section is going to cover paper more in depth.

First, prevent paper clutter by following our recommendations on junk mail and processing your incoming mail in Chapter 7. Less mail means less work!

As we also discussed in Chapter 7, there are essentially three kinds of paper: **A**ction, **R**eference and **T**rash. Remember the word "ART." Our "ART Chart" will help you know what to do with each type:

"The ART Chart" of Paper Management

3 Kinds of Paper	Types	What Does That Mean?	Examples	Where Do I Keep It?
A **"Action" Papers:** Some kind of action is needed.	**Quick Action**	Papers representing simple things you need to do; could be Urgent or Not-Urgent.	• Bills • Forms • Greeting cards • Addresses to enter • Receipts for a return • Something simple you're waiting on	Stacking trays work for most people; possibly small "piles" if that is your style; baskets; vertical sorters; or folders. These things must be triggered somewhere in your time management system to remind you to do them!
	Projects	Papers you are collecting in order to complete an action requiring multiple steps.	• Planning a party • Kids' activities • Remodeling projects • Business projects • Current year's income tax file	Usually a combination of hanging folders and manila folders in a drawer work best, sometimes bins if the project is large or bulky. Also manila folders in a wire desktop sorter.
R **"Reference" Papers:** You are just keeping them but don't need to take any action on them.	**Quick Reference**	Things you need to refer to quickly and often.	• Frequently called numbers list • School schedules • Lunch menus • Chores lists	Bulletin board, under glass on your desk, in your Family Binder (see our Communication Station "recipe"), attached to the back of a door, or stuck to your monitor (if items are small and few).
	Reference	Recent, relevant papers you need or want to save for later.	• Insurance paperwork • Home maintenance and warranty info • Medical information	Filing cabinets—we like lateral style (wide) cabinets best for better visibility to the whole row of files. You can file alphabetically or use categories and color-coding.
	Archives	An older version of Reference that you want to move out of your way. Seldom retrieved.	• Older tax records • Real estate documents • Older investment info	"Bankers Boxes" or plastic file box containers—"D" storage
T **Trash** We hope for a lot of this kind!	**Trash or Recycling**	Please recycle if you possibly can!	• Junk mail • Older catalogs and magazines	You may want a personal recycling bin near your own work area. Make sure your trash can is large enough to hold 2-3 days of trash! Petite, decorative bathroom cans need not apply!
	Shredding	Be sure to shred things that have account numbers or personal information.	• Credit card offers • Password information • Old financial records	You may want a personal shredding box near your work area if you have to take things elsewhere to shred.

Quick Actions

Establish permanent homes for the Quick Actions that are common to your situation. You can keep it simple and just have "Urgent" and "Not Urgent" if that works for you, but most people have a few of these common categories of Actions to set up:

- Address Book/Data Entry
- Bills
- Calls
- Discuss (can have a few of these for significant people)
- Errands
- Expense Reimbursements
- Financial Entry (Quicken, QuickBooks)
- House Projects
- Kids' Activities
- Medical Claims to Submit
- Medical Claims Pending
- Waiting (the only "action" is to wait for something else to happen first, such as having tickets to a play for next week)

Projects

Wire desktop sorters are recommended for your folders of Projects. They are great for keeping your projects visible and handy in an "A" location. If you have a small file drawer or desktop file box, you can use hanging folders with the manila folders inside to manage your Projects.

We like the Container Store's Elfa File Cart for a mobile solution for Quick Actions and Projects. You can use one color of hanging folders for the Quick Actions and one for the Projects to make a distinction. Then, store office supplies below in the drawers and roll this portable workstation around wherever you need it.

Reference—Your Filing System

Reference files contain information you may need to look at in the near future. Remember, nobody really ever taught any of us how to file—we all sort of learned by osmosis watching what our parents did or seeing how employers set up things in our first job. There really are many ways to file that are all correct as long as they work for you!

Most people file alphabetically and that usually makes sense in most situations. If you'd like to consider adding some categories and color-coding, keep a limit on the number of colors. It can make it difficult to file if you don't easily remember your colors and their meanings. A simple color-coding system might be green for financial, a favorite color for personal, and yellow for house and warranty-related files.

For help naming your files, consult our Common Household File Headings chart at the end of this "recipe." We usually separate car insurance files

What Do I Need to Keep?

This is one of the most commonly asked questions about paper management.

The general rule in the United States is that the IRS can go back as far as they want to investigate if they suspect fraud. However, the guideline of keeping seven years of tax-supporting documentation is generally accepted by most accountants and other experts.

You need to check with your own accountant or attorney to be sure about your particular situation.

from car maintenance files, but if you want to put it all together and call it "Car Stuff," that's okay. The key is that the names be **Meaningful** and **Memorable** so that you'll remember them when it's time to file again. Don't get too hung up on this decision! Just keep going and don't worry about doing it perfectly. It's better to have it done less-than-perfectly than not done at all! After you've decided, you may want to write a brief list of your file titles to create a File Index for yourself as a guideline moving forward.

For your monthly paid bills, receipts and statements, dispense with trying to file these alphabetically by vendor or account and try using a brown, January-December accordion file for the year's papers. We like the kind that are open-top (no flap closure) and already labeled with the months. Each month after you pay your bills and receive your regular account statements, file them quickly together in that month's section and be done with it. This system works for the majority of people and simplifies things greatly.

At least once a year, clean out your files, archive old reference material, and shred whatever you can. We recommend keeping the current and previous year's materials nearby in your filing cabinet and archiving older papers. Members of our program will be prompted on the weekly plans to do this at the right time.

Tried and True Products for Good Measure:
- We recommend lateral filing cabinets (the wide kind with the files running side to side). These allow the most visibility to your files and prevent the "reaching into the dark back of the drawer" problem. If you need to buy a cabinet, see if your city has a used office furniture store, as they often have excellent deals on good quality file cabinets.
- We also recommend using manila folders for initial sorting and hanging folders for keeping the papers in your filing cabinet. Hanging folders keep the files orderly so they won't fall all over each other and

slump down in the drawer. They do require having the proper rails in your file drawer. Most quality filing cabinets come with this capability, but if for some reason you need the rails, purchase inexpensive ones at any office supply store, assemble them, and drop them into the drawers. We recommend buying high-quality, brand-name hanging folders, since the cheaper ones will fall apart over time. The glue will loosen on the metal rails and they will slide out.

- Many people do not know about "box-bottom" files. These folders are made for bulky files to keep them from bulging in the drawer and obscuring the view of the other tabs. You can get them in 1-, 2-, or 3-inch widths. We usually use 2-inch ones.

Common Household File Headings

File Content Category	Suggested Titles	Comments
Bank Statements	"(bank name) Checking (year)" or "(bank name) Savings (year)"	Preferably filed with paid bills in a Jan-Dec accordion file. Strongly consider getting these statements electronically from their website and requesting paperless communication! If you do want these in with your main files, naming the folders by year and separating them out this way makes it easier to archive later.
Brokerage Statements	"Brokerage Statements 2005," 2006, 2007, etc., or investment company such as "Schwab (year)" or "Merrill Lynch (year)"	Strongly consider getting these statements electronically from their website and requesting paperless communication! Naming the folders by year and separating them out this way makes it easier to archive later.
Cars/Vehicles	"Chrysler Pacifica" (your car's make/model)	Contains all papers about initial purchase, registration, inspections, repairs, and other things unique to that vehicle. Separate the insurance and loan information into other folders (see Insurance, Loans). Keep the title in your Fire Safe (see Fire Safe).
Cards & Keepsakes	"Keepsakes-(name of person)" or "Memorabilia-(name of person)"	One folder for each family member- may need a bin rather than a folder if you like keeping a lot.

File Content Category	Suggested Titles	Comments
Career Planning	"Career Planning-(name of person)"	Resumes, performance reviews, goals, educational transcripts.
Child Care Information	"(name of child care provider/center)" or "Child Care" or "Babysitter Info"	Can also keep this in your Family Binder. Includes general information about day care policies and procedures and correspondence, or a list of babysitters' numbers and identification information.
Churches/Places of Worship, Clubs	"(name of organization)"	Contains general reference information about policies and other membership data.
Credit Card Information	"MBNA Credit Card Account Info" (for specific account) or more generally, "Credit Card Info"	Recommended to save terms & conditions agreements and correspondence about the account itself (not the statements) in this file. Usually okay to put different accounts' information together in one file since there may not be much for each.
Credit Card Statements	Recommended to file with paid bills in accordion file, but if not, title "MBNA Credit Card (year)" (your bank name + year)	File in Jan-Dec accordion file with paid bills instead of in the main files. Strongly consider getting these statements electronically from their website and requesting paperless communication! If you do file in your main files, naming the folders by year and separating them out this way makes it easier to archive later.
Credit Reports	"Credit Reports"	We remind our paid members to run these reports 3x a year. It's generally okay to shred the oldest one when you put a new one in the file. Keep the last year's reports for reference, unless there is a problem on one of them, in which case you will want to keep until the problem is resolved.
Death or Family Information	"(name of loved one who has passed)" or "(Family Last Name) Information"	If you have planned a funeral or been involved in the loss of a loved one, you may have information that is important to keep. Death certificates are better kept under "Identification" or in a Fire Safe.
Decorating Ideas	"House Ideas," "Decorating Ideas" or other as you prefer	Contains clippings of things you like for your house, such as furniture or paint ideas. If you have a lot of these, you may want to make an accordion folder just for this, separated with divisions by room. Could be a project file if you are actively redecorating.

File Content Category	Suggested Titles	Comments
Financial Planning	"Financial Planning," "Retirement Planning"	Contains general information about planning your investments, notes on any advice you've received, Social Security statements, or articles related to this subject.
Fire Safe or Safe Deposit Box	(not a folder)	Having a fire safe or safe deposit box is a good idea for original documents that are difficult to replace, such as birth certificates, original deeds, and vehicle titles. Home inventory records are important too. Make copies of these documents to put into your Identification file for quicker access to the information.
Gift Certificates & Gift Cards	"Gift Certificates"	Have a file for temporary storage of gift certificates you haven't used. Set up a reminder as some go out of date.
Gifts, Gift Ideas	"Gift Ideas" or "Gifts"	Ideas, lists and clippings from catalogs related to gifts you have given or might like to give.
Health & Nutrition	"Health & Fitness" or "Nutrition" or "Wellness"	Contains articles of interest about health and exercise and nutrition.
Holidays	"Christmas" or "Hanukkah" or other major holidays for your family	Contains information about previous years' completed plans for future reference. Active plans for this year can be a Project folder and relevant information can move here when finished.
Home Improvements & Repairs	"Home Improvements" or "(street name of your house) Home Improvements"	Keep receipts here for major home improvements and repairs, along with general information about your home's maintenance. No need to keep minor receipts such as exterminator services or carpet cleaning, unless there are termites involved or other issues beyond routine matters.
Humor	"Funny File," "Humor"	Your "Funny File" contains funny comic strip clippings, printouts of jokes, and other fun things people have shared with you.
Identification & Legal Papers	"Identification"	Voter registration cards, copies of birth certificates, marriage certificates and passports (keep originals in a fire safe if possible- see Fire Safe).

File Content Category	Suggested Titles	Comments
Income Tax	"Income Tax (year)" or "Taxes (year)"	One for each year, make some in advance. Include all papers that were directly used to prepare the return, such as W-2s and 1099 year-end statements, any IRS correspondence, and also a copy of the return itself.
Inspirations & Quotes	"Inspirations & Quotes," "Inspirations," "Spiritual"	You may like collecting favorite quotations or clippings of articles and stories that you relate to on a personal or spiritual level.
Insurance	Keep separate files for "Insurance-Auto," "Insurance-Property," "Insurance-Medical," "Insurance-Life," and "Insurance-Other"	Keep your policies and most recent correspondence here for each category. Ask for paperless options! For medical, you may need to have Project files that are for active papers, such as "Medical Claims to Be Filed" and "Medical Claims Pending." This folder is for general information and completed issues.
Inventory	"Home Inventory" or "Inventory"	If you have taken a home inventory, keep the most current list here, and a copy in your fire safe or safe deposit box.
Investment Information	"Stocks," "Investments," or "(name of particular stock, bond, or fund)"	For general information and correspondence about your investments. You might want to split this into various folders if you have a lot of them. This is not for the statements; those need to be done separately (see Brokerage Statements).
Loans	"Bank of America Car Loan," "Chevrolet Loan" (your information as you will remember it)	Contains all loan papers and correspondence for that account. Recommended to request paperless statements, or file statements in Jan-Dec accordion file with bills.
Maps & Directions	"Maps & Directions"	Contains driving directions and maps for things you will likely visit again. If you just have a few, you can file under "Travel- Places We've Been."
Medical	"Medical-(name of person)"	Medical history, important test results, medical records, vaccinations/shot records for each person in the family.

File Content Category	Suggested Titles	Comments
Mortgage	"(street name of your house) Mortgage"	Contains correspondence and other general information about your home loan. It is suggested that you get a paperless statement instead of saving your statements each month—if you prefer paper, we suggest filing it in the Jan-Dec accordion file with paid bills, since it's a routine expense. If your closing documents are too large, you can archive them or store them on a bookshelf in a magazine holder.
Neighborhood Association	"(name of neighborhood/ subdivision)"	Contains information about your neighborhood covenants and restrictions, a handbook or directory, pool and club information if applicable.
Personal Style	"Image" or "Hair Ideas" or "Fashion" or "Personal Style"	A place you can save clippings of fashion, hair and makeup ideas, if you have them.
Pet Information	"(name of pet)," "Pet Info"	If you have more than one pet, you will probably want to name the folder by the pet's name. Contains vet bills and medical history, registration papers, pedigree, etc.
Property Taxes	"Property Tax" or "(name of street of your house)- Property Tax"	Keep each year's property tax statement and all related correspondence. It's good to keep them all together since you can look at them comparatively.
Restaurant Ideas	"Restaurants" or "Dining Out"	Ideas and clippings about restaurants you'd like to try, including that article of the "Ten Best Desserts" in your city, for example!
School	"(name of school)"	Can also keep this in family binder—just general information about school policies, student handbook.
Special Interests	Assign title according to interests, such as "Camping," "Parenting," "Waterskiing," "Genealogy," etc.	Contains articles of interest, notes from seminars about that subject, information about equipment you might need for it, etc.
Things to Do	"Things to Do" or "Travel- Local Places" or "Activities" or "Recreation"	Ideas and clippings about local/regional activities you and guests can do on a weekend or even day trips in your area.

File Content Category	Suggested Titles	Comments
Travel	We recommend two main folders—"Travel- Places We've Been," and "Travel- Places We'd Like to Go"	Keep your ideas here for future travel, as well as brochures, maps, and directions for places you've been in case you want to go back or tell someone else about them.
Travel Reward Programs	"Frequent Flyer Programs" or "Mileage Programs" or "Travel Reward Programs"	Contains latest statements about your airline, hotel and rental car points. No need to keep past statements, just throw out the oldest one when you add a new one. You probably don't need separate folders for all of them. Also, strongly consider requesting paperless statements for these programs.
Trophies	"Trophies-(name of person)"	An optional file that I like to call Trophies, but you can call it something else you like. It contains achievements you are particularly proud of, like an important thank-you note from a customer, an article about you in the newspaper, a copy of your first check received in your business, or a certificate for an award.
Warranties & Instructions	"Warranties- Appliances, Other" "Warranties- Art & Décor" "Warranties- Computer/Peripherals" "Warranties- Furniture" "Warranties- Jewelry" "Warranties- Kids' Toys" "Warranties- Kitchen" "Warranties- Major Appliances" "Warranties- Outdoor/Garage" "Warranties- Personal/Health" "Warranties- Small Electronics" "Warranties- Sports & Exercise" "Warranties- TV/DVD/VCR"	These are suggested categories. If you don't have many warranties, you can get away with using a separate accordion file labeled with these categories to keep all of this together. Most homeowners find that they will use these as separate files. They need to be reviewed and purged each time you access them. For computer manuals and disks that came with your machine when you bought it, it's a good idea to bundle these together with a zip lock bag before filing to make sure you know which things go with which computer. Alternatively, you can store these computer items together in a binder case on a shelf, since they are often bulky.

Bathrooms

Ingredients for Success:

The bathroom is one of my favorite rooms to organize, because the contents are straightforward and easy to categorize. The main functions in this room are:

- **Bathing** (toiletries, robes and towels)
- **Grooming/Personal Care** (toiletries, cosmetics and medications)
- **Dressing** (clothing and hampers may be here or nearby)

You're going to have items you use daily, almost more than any other items in your home, like your toothbrush and hairbrush. **We usually set up an operating supply of these items (your "A" and "B" stuff), then create a backstock of refill items for each category, like a little "convenience store" of items in the cabinets.**

When reviewing the items, we tend to sort them by parts of the body, such as teeth, hair, nails, skin care, etc. Here are the most common categories:

- Dental Care
- Hair Care
- Skin Care
- Makeup (subdivided by cheeks, eyes, lips)
- Shaving
- First Aid
- Soaps
- Travel Items
- Paper Goods (cotton balls, tissue, swabs)
- Ear, Nose & Throat Medications
- Medications by person

Create an every day drawer for each person, containing the "A" and "B" items that they use most often. If you are short on drawer space, use baskets or shelves to achieve the same goal. I have used beautiful glass bowls to hold every day items, too.

A Pinch of This and a Dash of That:

Organizing a bathroom is really easy because many of the items are dated! We wish that all clutter had expiration dates on it. I have a client who is a pharmaceutical consultant, and she says you really should discard expired medications and toiletries, as the dates are there for a good reason. (See "Get Your Greens" on the next page for proper disposal suggestions.)

Remember your paper and pen when you are getting ready to organize a bathroom, because you will likely need to replace some expired items and will want to write them down.

Many of us are confused about all of the product claims out there, and we buy things to help us look younger and feel better without really knowing if they work. Sometimes these purchases add up and result in a giant glut of products we are not using but feel bad about throwing away (as they are often expensive). We love www.cosmeticscop.com for product reviews to help decide which skin and hair products are worth the hype.

Unless the bottles are unopened, charity groups will not typically want them, and even if originally sealed, you should check with the intended recipient before donating. Homeless shelters definitely love to receive travel-sized items like the ones from hotels. You might be able to give products that are already opened to a friend or family member to prevent wasting them. But discard your unused products if you have not used them in about a year, so that what you keep is safe, effective, and justifies the storage space it occupies.

Your goal in organizing the bathroom is to make it as easy as possible for you to get dressed and ready for your day. Keep this in mind as you mull over the products you don't use but are continuing to store—are they just in the way? Would it be easier if they were gone? What is the worst thing that could happen if you didn't have them?

Get Your Greens

Discarding medications requires additional precautions. Despite the movies and television shows you've seen where people are flushing pills down the toilet, that disposal method is an extremely bad idea as it pollutes our water supply. If your local pharmacy or hazardous waste disposal department has a return program, that is the best way to handle these drugs. Otherwise, it's recommended by authorities to dispose of drugs in the trash after modifying them to discourage consumption by other humans or wild animals. You can add water or other liquids to pills and shake up the bottle to dissolve them. Add flour or salt or other dry compounds to liquid medications to absorb them, and wrap blister-packs of pills with duct tape. It's also suggested that you disguise drugs in the trash by putting them inside other containers, and you should scratch off or mark over your name and prescription number for safety as well.

Tried and True Products for Good Measure:

- **Under sink shelving units:** Pipes under the sink often complicate the utilization of cabinet storage. We like using an inexpensive under sink shelving unit, sold at Organize.com and also found at Target, that assembles around the pipes inside the cabinet. No tools are required—it simply snaps together and uses thumbscrews that are easy to hand-tighten. Once you use this product to create a couple of levels of shelving, then add small bins on the shelves and pull them out like drawers as needed. You can create up to three levels of shelving in a typical under sink cabinet and get up to eight or nine little "drawers" in a normally wasted space. These bins can be labeled with the categories of your back stocked items, such as Hair Care, Skin Care, Travel Items, and so on.

- **Sterilite #1622 bins:** These bins are perfect for using on the under sink shelving units mentioned above. You can get these at most major discount stores.

- **Plastic drawer units:** Measure the cabinet first and find a set of plastic drawers that fit in the space. These are found at any major discount store in a wide variety of sizes.

- **Tension pole storage shelves for the bath or shower:** Add storage to the bathtub or shower itself by installing these simple shelving units that work the same way as a tension shower curtain rod. Measure first, as always, to make sure the height of your ceiling will work with the product you purchase, and buy a high quality product that will not rust or crack easily. Alternatively, you can purchase a caddy that hangs over the shower head to hold extra toiletries.

- **Etagere units for over the commode:** Many major stores carry lines of bathroom storage units, including these over-toilet cabinets. You can use them to store extra towels or toiletries, and they are available in a variety of materials and colors to match your decor.

- **Hinge-It Invisible Valet:** I have found that many homes are lacking enough towel-hanging space. This towel rack installs easily using the hinge pins on your existing door, and it provides space for several towels to hang behind the door. You can see a photo of this product where we have used it to store toilet paper as well, on my blog at http://budurl.com/towelrack. You can purchase them at www.hingeit.com.

Bedrooms

Ingredients for Success:

The bedroom is primarily for sleeping and relaxing. Yet, it often becomes a "Stressed Out Space" (see Chapter 10), with too many other competing functions crowding the room. Make sure these functions are not interfering with your ability to rest comfortably.

Here are the major functions of a bedroom:

- Sleeping (bed, pillows, linens, lamps)
- Reading (books, magazines, glasses, highlighters, pens)
- Dressing (clothing and hampers)
- Grooming (hair styling and makeup application, if not done in the bathroom)
- Television/Music/Computer (CDs, DVDs and other media, remote controls, software, gaming gear)
- Toy Storage/Play Area—for children's rooms (more on toys in the Family Room/Playroom recipe pages)

You may have other hobbies, like practicing a musical instrument, that you enjoy in this space. Create a station for those supplies as well.

The features of the bedroom are typically large furniture pieces like a bed, a dresser, nightstands and chairs. As you take on this project, stop to consider whether rearranging the furniture would help with the flow of activities in the room. If you are sharing the room, would it benefit you both to create zones for each of your activities?

We like to start organizing a bedroom by making the bed. This gives us a nice flat surface for sorting, using the centralizing method we discussed in Chapter 11.

A Pinch of This and a Dash of That:

Hotel rooms are simple and refreshing. They efficiently contain all of the necessary functions of a bedroom within a very small space. I am often inspired by this when traveling—at how simply one can live without anything extra required. Use this concept as motivation as you make decisions about what to keep in your room.

Make your bed daily. Your mother was right. It is a small gift you can give yourself each morning that you will appreciate throughout the day. Your room appears neater and more organized instantly, and it is so much more inviting to climb into a bed that is made!

If you store your clothing in bureau drawers, consider whether that clothing is better stored in your closet, if this is possible. Many times we have moved a dresser into a walk-in closet to centralize all of the client's clothing in one area. That way someone can get out of the shower and not have to go to two different places to get underwear, socks and clothes. Obviously this won't work if you have a reach-in closet or if your dresser is very large.

If you are an avid reader, make sure your bedside table supports your habit by providing adequate storage. If you have only a table without additional levels of shelving, consider something else that will work better to hold lots of reading material underneath, or add a small bookcase nearby.

If you are trying to operate a home office from your bedroom, consider that it may interfere with your ability to rest adequately. If you must include your office operations as a function of your bedroom space, try to separate the spaces with a folding screen, a furniture piece or curtain if possible. You can also try this approach for other major competing functions like a nursery or exercise space.

Tried and True Products for Good Measure:
- **Underbed storage containers:** Feng Shui experts will disagree with my recommendation, but there is a lot of great storage space under the bed. Utilize it properly with containers so that small things don't get lost and you can pull it all out easily. Any major discount store carries these long, flat containers. They are great for gift wrap, seasonal clothing such as sweaters, and extra shoes.

- **Toy hammocks:** These mesh hammocks can hold a lot of stuffed animals and other toys and get them off the floor and the bed. You can find them at any toy store and some discount stores, or search online for "toy hammocks." Organize.com has one that comes with both hooks and suction cups, so that it can be used in the bathtub for drying and storing bath toys.

- **Bed organizer pockets:** These pockets tuck in between the mattress and box spring and hang beside the bed to hold items like glasses, pens, puzzle books and remote controls. You can easily make them yourself if you are so inclined, or you can buy them online by searching "bedside organizer" or "bed organizer."

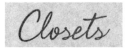

Closets

Ingredients for Success:

It's a fact that most people start and end the day in their closets. I am convinced that the state of a person's closet has a subtle but great effect on the quality of their life and work. **You want to start each day with a closet full of easily visible clothes and accessories that fit and flatter you—now—and make you feel terrific.**

The first stumbling blocks are often the questions of whether to hire a closet company, and how. Homebuilders typically put in one simple rod and shelf, and companies like California Closets can make drastic improvements. Do you really need a closet company, and how do you choose which one to work with?

Whether you hire a closet company or not, the smart thing to do is organize your existing closet contents yourself first. When a closet company comes to do an estimate, they count how many shoes and handbags there are and measure the linear feet of shelving and hanging space that you require. They then design a custom closet around what you have. It doesn't make sense for them to construct a closet around a bunch of stuff you never use, so the first thing to do is go through all of the clothing, shoes and accessories and decide what will stay.

Once you see what is left, you may realize that you don't need a new closet since you've pared down so much, or if you still have a problem, at least now the closet will be designed around what you truly use and need.

If you decide to continue down the path toward a custom closet, research those companies that will come to your home for free to do a design and estimate. They may need to schedule another appointment with you to present the designs. Have all decision-makers on hand for that meeting so you can decide whether to move forward. It will take several weeks, typically, to cut the parts for your design and schedule the installers. You can spend anywhere from a few hundred dollars to several thousand, depending upon the features you want.

Questions to Ask the Closet Company:

- How long have you been in business? Are you a franchisee?
- What warranty do you offer? Does it apply only to me, or future owners of my home?
- What colors do you have available for the melamine (laminate) material?
- Is the melamine thermal-fused or cold processed? Thermal-fused melamine wears much better.
- Is the particleboard furniture grade or industrial grade? Industrial grade holds the screws better and is thicker.
- Is there any plastic used in the hardware? Metal parts are preferred.
- What is the standard shelf depth you use? Builders' standard is 11.5 inches, but having deeper shelves such as 14" or 16" is greatly preferred for holding larger sweaters and even suitcases.

- How are your drawer units constructed? How is the drawer handle hardware fastened? Are full extension glides included? Full extension glides provide the best support for your drawers and are a good idea, even if it is an upgrade. Construction of drawers can be a big differentiator in quality.

- Do you offer oval clothing rods? Just like an egg's oval shape provides strength, chrome oval-shaped clothing rods are stronger than rounded ones. Metal rods are usually a better choice than wooden ones.

- Does your installation include tearing out the old closet? Will you do wall repairs and touch-up painting?

- What accessories do you offer, and how much are they? Is there an alternative to these accessories? You will see accessories like valet rods, shoe fences, sliding belt racks, sliding tie racks, jewelry trays, acrylic shelf dividers, hampers, pull-out ironing boards, pull-down upper clothing rods, and many others. They are all great, but you need to watch how the cost might add up.

Just like buying a car, there are standard features and there are upgrades, whether in quality of construction or in additional accessories. If you're prepared and ask a lot of good questions, you'll end up with a great closet for the best price.

Organizing Your Existing Closet

First pick up any clothing on the floor and get laundry started while you work. Sort through the clothing, shoes, and accessories using the concepts you've learned in previous chapters. If you have a separate garment rack available, it can be a helpful tool in the sorting process. Make lists as you go of action items that result, items to buy to complete the project, and new wardrobe items that you need to purchase.

Be realistic and honest with yourself. Avoid the traps of keeping things that are too large or small, out of style, or unflattering in fit or color. If you can have a friend help with this project, all the better for getting an objective opinion on that purple mini-dress.

After reviewing your items, you will likely end up with all or most of these categories:

- Keep—clothing, shoes, and accessories that fit and flatter you right now
- Trash—torn or stained items that are unwearable
- Donations—for charity
- Give to Friends—items you would like someone special to have
- Alterations & Repairs—items that can be worn again with a little help
- Consignment/Garage Sale—items you'd like to sell instead of donate
- Seasonal—items that need to be stored for another season (or another size!)
- Elsewhere—unrelated items that belong somewhere else and need to be put away

Next, sort the clothing you're keeping by season, then by type, sleeve length and color. Think of it as "filing" your clothes. Some people may prefer sorting by casual, career, and formal clothing as well. People in warmer climates may not need to sort by season. In Austin, Texas, for example, winter weather is so variable we never know if we'll need to wear shorts or a parka.

Usage determines storage. Prioritize placement of your items by the frequency of their use (A-B-C-D). If you use it often, make it more accessible.

Are you up for the Imelda Marcos Award? Lots of women I know collect shoes like kids collect rocks or Barbies or bugs. Use our A-B-C-D prioritizing method to think through how you use your shoes. Which shoes are your favorites that you wear all the time? Which ones pinch your feet and hurt but you really have to wear them with this one matching outfit?

Take the "D" shoes and donate them to charity. Your "C" shoes are special shoes that are seldom worn. Put these up higher and possibly into clear shoeboxes to protect them from dust. By the way, in most situations, we do not believe in putting all shoes into shoeboxes. It is inefficient for "A" and "B" shoes to be stored that way—it takes two hands to put them away and they are often stacked and hard to pull out.

Your "A" and "B" shoes should be totally accessible, near eye level or below so you can reach them and put them away easily. You will likely want to sort them by color, such as all black shoes together, or by formality or season. This is a personal preference; decide what makes sense for you.

A Pinch of This and a Dash of That:

Create a place to put empty hangers together so you can find them easily. When you remove a piece of clothing, make a habit of placing the empty hanger in this reserved spot.

Don't ignore blank wall space and the backs of doors. Use hooks and take up all of the spare space you can, even if you only hang up hats and other small items.

Add another level of shelving if possible. Most builders do not install additional shelves beyond the initial rod and shelf, and many homes have much higher ceilings and can accommodate a great deal more. Modular units will often do the trick if you don't want to install permanent shelves. If your ceiling is high enough, you might even be able to add a third level of hanging rods for seasonal clothing.

If you have only one clothing rod, adding a second level below will double your hanging space. This strategy works great if you have a lot of short-hanging items like shirts and pants. You may be able to add a second level part-way and still leave about two linear feet of rod space for long-hanging items.

Move your clothing to make the closet work better. As we mentioned in the Bedroom recipe pages, consider moving your dresser into or nearer to the closet to centralize your clothing. If you have another closet or storage space available, move seasonal items elsewhere to make room for only currently usable clothing. In the case that you are trying to lose or gain weight or are moving in and out of maternity wear, you may want to locate your larger or smaller clothing in a section of its own. You want to make it as easy as possible to choose each day.

Shoe Tips:
- For measuring shelf capacity for shoes, the width of a pair of women's shoes is approximately 6.5 inches and men's are approximately 9 inches.
- The average woman owns 40 pairs of shoes.
- For tall boots, insert a rolled up magazine or catalog as a boot stay to keep them from flopping over. No need to buy those plastic boot stays from specialty stores.

Tried and True Products for Good Measure:

- **Matching hangers:** Purchasing matching hangers is a "secret" of Professional Organizers. Clear acrylic hangers with swivel heads are a good choice, as well as white tubular or wooden hangers. We are serious about this! It can make a huge difference in the way your closet looks and feels. Your local discount store will have a great price on these.

- **Shelf dividers:** These acrylic or chrome dividers slide right onto your shelves to keep stacks from toppling over. They are great for sweaters, sweatshirts, pants, and other stacks of clothing on a shelf. You can find a great selection online at OrganizeIt.com, LillianVernon.com and StacksAndStacks.com.

- **Simple Division® Garment Organizers:** Organize your closet like the pros—this is our own product and a bestseller! These plastic dividers allow you to create sections of clothing in your closet so you can stay organized. Our most popular labels are "Too Big" and "Too Small." The dividers are also great for kids who share a closet, and they help to manage hand-me-downs. 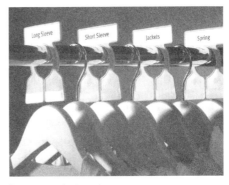 You can even use them to separate which clothing needs ironing or create a section for uniforms or other unique needs. Our dividers are specially shaped to allow wide, flat labeling space across the top, and they are designed not to spin around on the rod like round ones do. They come in 12-packs that include 60 labels in English and Spanish, or buy them in our bulk Professional Packs of 50 at ClutterDiet.com.

- **Overdoor hanging shoe bags:** I like these for many things other than just shoes—they are great for toys and baby supplies, too. I prefer the kind made of clear plastic so you can see what is in the pockets. Some of these bags are available that hang from the closet rod as opposed to the back of the door. You can get these at any discount store.

- **Valet rods:** One of my favorite accessories is a telescoping valet rod, which gives you a place to stage clothing for packing or put up the dry cleaning when you get it home. I use mine daily to pick out what I am going to wear and also use it when pressing with a steamer. You can buy these online at ClosetValet.com and Organize-It-Online.com.

- **Stackable shoe shelves:** We like the "Organize It" line of laminate ones sold at Target and other discount stores. We do not, however, like the modular cubicle units that are sold for shoes—in which each shoe or pair of shoes supposedly fits into a small cubbyhole. Women's shoes do not usually fit well into these cubbies, you cannot see them very well, and men's shoes especially do not fit. Instead of a cubby approach, use shelves, since they are much more versatile.

- **"Shoes Away" bag:** The Shoes Away shoe bag is one of those "as seen on TV" products that actually works. It will hold 30 pairs of shoes in a small space, and you can hang it over the back of a door. Look for the best price online by searching "Shoes Away."

- **Elfa closet systems:** The Container Store's Elfa products are ingeniously designed and extremely high in quality. I can install them myself, which really says something for their ease of use. Elfa is a great do-it-yourself option.

- **Jewelry armoires:** These range in size from fantastic countertop chests to larger furniture pieces that hold all of your jewelry in one place and make it visible and easy to choose. Search online for "jewelry armoires" for a large selection.

- **Scarf hangers:** These plastic items look like large, solid, sturdy hangers with holes in them. You poke your scarves through the holes and the entire thing hangs from your clothing rod. Available at the Container Store.

- **Belt and tie hooks and hangers:** If you have wall space, hang a set of belt hooks up for your belts and ties; if you don't have wall space, use belt hangers. These are hangers that have a row of hooks across the bottom to sort your belts. They are available at any discount store.

Communication Station

Ingredients for Success:

The elements of a good Communication Station are:

- **Message Space:** A whiteboard, chalkboard or paper and pens for phone messages and other communications and reminders.

- **Mail and Paper Distribution:** Trays, cubbies or bins for each family member's mail and messages, if needed.

- **Family Calendar:** A centralized calendar where all family activities can be consolidated and viewed. We recommend a paper calendar with large squares.

- **Posting Space:** A corkboard, magnet board or similar display area to keep important information.
- **Family Binder:** This is the best place to put all of your family's important information that you need on a daily basis. You can keep it in a common area like your kitchen or your home office.

The Family Binder is "Command Central" for all of the commonly-needed information in your home. It might contain frequently called numbers, soccer schedules, church phone lists, medical information, babysitter phone numbers, school schedules, calendars, and MUCH, MUCH more. Your imagination is the limit. What are your family members always asking you to find? "Mo-o-om! Where's the swim team's schedule?" "Mo-o-om! Where's Grandma's phone number?" I am sure you can think of all kinds of things to put in here!

You need a large 3-ring binder and some sturdy dividers, preferably with pockets. They do sell extra-wide dividers now that will easily stick out beyond page protector sheets, so you might also look for that feature. **Below are some suggested categories and ideas for things you can put in your binder.**

Administration/Activities:
- Frequently Called Numbers page with Emergency Numbers on it
- Family master calendar
- Weekly Overview Chart of your family's activities (from your workbook)
- Family phone directory (can print out your Outlook address book for reference)
- Passwords and account information (if you are comfortable having it here)
- Phone lists for various organizations and classes

- Schedules for activities such as sports and clubs
- School holiday calendar
- Shopping Lists for groceries, discount stores and bulk purchases
- Wish Lists of books to read and videos to rent

Child Care:
- Sitter reference information (meals, snacks, naps, rules)
- Carpool and day care information
- Time sheets for sitters or nannies
- Petty cash account tracking sheet for sitters or nannies
- Task list for sitters or nannies

Cleaning & Maintenance:
- Cleaning schedules and checklists
- Indoor maintenance checklists
- Outdoor maintenance checklists
- Light bulb chart
- Car VIN numbers and license plate numbers
- Car maintenance records
- Recycling and trash service reference information
- Storage inventory lists
- Home inventory information

Events & Holidays:
- Perpetual birthday calendar
- Birthday party checklist
- Entertaining checklist
- Holiday card list
- Holiday planning notes
- Wish Lists for holidays and birthdays
- Gift Ideas List
- Clothing sizes

Health & Safety:

- Map to nearest hospital
- Medical insurance information
- Vaccination records
- Medical information and treatment permission forms for sitters
- Allergy and other important health information
- Pets' health information

Meals:

- Menu planning forms
- School lunch menu
- List of favorite breakfasts
- List of favorite school lunches
- List of favorite dinners
- Rotation menu for dinners
- List of meals in the freezer to use

Travel:

- Packing Lists
- Leaving Town Checklist
- Camping Checklist
- Picnic/Outdoor Events Checklist
- Places We'd Like to Go list
- House-sitter and Pet-sitter Information

Other Options:

- Sheet protectors for important pages
- Business card holders to keep frequently-called vendors' cards handy
- Zippered pouch to hold pens, sticky notes and other supplies

Can Keep On the Computer:

- Master address book in your favorite contact manager, such as Outlook

- Home Inventory (use a form of your own or try ASafeSpot.com or Eprooft.com)
- Passwords and account information (Try Splash ID from www. splashid.com or Password Agent for Windows at www.moonsoftware.com)

A Pinch of This and a Dash of That:

Of course, another element is communication itself! Make sure the whole family knows that this Communication Station exists and that is where they are to leave messages and find information.

You can try color-coding family activities on your calendar using a different colored marker or pen for each family member. Office supply stores sell large write-on, wipe-off laminated calendars, which can be a good choice. You do have to erase them however, and rewrite the numbers once a month, and they don't provide a written record for referring back later. We recommend paper calendars instead.

Tried and True Products for Good Measure:

- **Cozi.com:** If you are technically inclined, this free family calendar option might work well for you. It includes the text message shopping list option we discussed in Chapter 15.
- **Pottery Barn's "Daily System: "** This set of organizing products hangs from a bar across the wall and can be switched out as needed. Choose from a corkboard, a whiteboard, a magnetic chalkboard, a recharging station, mail cubbies and other modules. They look and work great.

Creation Station (Arts and Crafts Supplies)

Ingredients for Success:

If you've ever felt the creative urge to whip out some old fabric and sew a skirt, but then quickly felt the air deflate out of your creative bubble because you had to search for that sewing machine foot, a zipper, and... where did that fabric get stashed away...? You need to get your creative space organized!

Designating a space for your craft supplies is key. Make sure there is a large flat work surface and plenty of light. For some, this can be a shelf in a closet near your kitchen table. For others, it will be one section of a room. If you're fortunate enough to have an entire room dedicated to your creative endeavors, consider having open shelving instead of cabinets for your supplies. For many artistic people, visibility is what inspires you and reminds you of what supplies you have. Out of sight really is out of mind. To keep these shelves looking uncluttered, use clear plastic containers to corral each category of supplies. Label each container so you can quickly find what you want.

Set up zones for different types of functions needed in the space. With sewing, for example, you may need zones for pressing, cutting and using the machine.

When deciding how to organize your craft supplies, think about the "Limiting Container" idea we've talked about before. If you have so much Elmer's glue that you can't fit it all in one container, get rid of the excess. It costs more in terms of storage space and your energy to keep all that glue (or any other supply you have in excess) than it's worth. Let the craft stores warehouse all that stuff for you.

After you've decided what supplies you're going to keep, **sort them by putting like items together in labeled containers.** Keep all fabrics together, all paints together, all rubber stamps together, etc.

A Pinch of This and a Dash of That:

Be realistic about which crafts you're really passionate and likely to work on. Don't keep every needlepoint kit you've ever bought just because someday you might have the time to do one—especially if your real passion is painting! Dedicate your space to storing the supplies that really inspire you and let go of the supplies that you'll probably never use. Donate them to a school, church or daycare that will use them.

We recommend having "project drawers" or bins for each project you're working on, so all of the related supplies are contained together to do the work. For example, a new dress project bin would contain the pattern, the cut pieces, the thread and the notions that are needed to work on it. Additionally, this method allows you to see (and limit) how many projects you have going concurrently.

Check out what the pros are doing for your particular hobby. If you are into quilting, see how the quilting shops store their equipment and supplies. You will be able to adopt some of these products and methods in your own workspace.

Tried and True Products for Good Measure:
- **Plastic drawers:** Sometimes we use plastic drawers for projects, available at any discount store. These drawers are also great for supplies, since they have wheels and are mobile to store away in a closet and bring out when you need them.

- **"Fishing tackle" boxes:** There are all kinds of art supply cases that have small compartments for sorting various colors of thread and other needs. Craft stores carry lots of options for hobby-specific needs, but also check your hardware store for tool and hardware cases that may work just as well and cost less.

- **Tilt-bins:** These modular units can be purchased online or at hardware stores, and they hold various kinds of art supplies for scrapbooking and other crafts. You can mount them easily on the wall and keep adding more.

- **Magnetic knife strips:** These work great for knives in the kitchen, and in a craft area you can use them to keep scissors and other tools handy. Search "magnetic knife strips" online to find some online, or find them at the Container Store.

- **Many other organizing products for specific crafts are found at your local craft store.** You might be surprised at the inventive ideas for storing items particular to your hobby!

Destination Station (Entry and Exit Area)

Ingredients for Success:

The Destination Station should be set up in the place where you and your family enter and exit the house and put things down. This area is a constant maintenance issue for most families' homes.

You can set up Destination Stations in various ways...consider using a shelf for each family member, a cubby system, hooks, a special piece of furniture such as a sideboard or armoire, or any other clever method that will work for your home's configuration. Create this area in a place closest to where you enter and exit, but if you enter into a narrow hallway, you might want to set it up in the room closest to where you enter, such as a laundry room.

Here are the elements of a good Destination Station:

- **Errand shelf:** A place to put things to be returned to other places or people. Videos, library books, store return items, and borrowed things can go here and wait to be collected when you leave. These items may also be kept in your car, if you cannot find a place for an errand shelf.

- **Key hooks:** Hang up hooks for your keys so you will have a home for them right when you walk in. Decorative accessory stores now sell the kinds of hooks that look really attractive in your home and complement your personal style. You can also use a beautiful pottery bowl or dish to hold your keys if that works better.

- **Family baggage:** Purses, backpacks and briefcases all need a home here. Since you are doing this work, give yourself first pick at the best shelf.

- **Cellular phones & pagers:** Leave these here and set them up to charge when you come in so they don't get lost in the house.

- **Incoming & outgoing mail:** A possible location, but another may fit your situation better. A wastebasket is helpful here for this purpose.

- **Equipment for regular lessons or practices:** musical instruments, sports gear or other items needed regularly.

- **Small "purse refill" items:** Gum, mints, tissues, lotions

- **Sunglasses:** Now they have a home!

- **Shoes and socks for kids:** It is efficient to have these ready by the door to go out; otherwise children need to go to their rooms to put on shoes and that process can take much longer, especially for young children.

- **Coats and scarves:** if necessary and possible in your space

- **Bench:** for taking off/putting on shoes or boots

You can get really creative with these elements, and sometimes you must. We have taken underutilized coat closets and turned them into full Destination Stations just by removing some hanging space and adding a shelf for each person and for errands. We have also used a buffet or sideboard storage piece and made the drawers serve these needs.

A Pinch of This and a Dash of That:

Charging stations are becoming more important with the additional gadgets we are all carrying. Housewares and furniture catalogs are coming up with great charger station products. We've been known to drill holes into the back of furniture pieces to run cords into a drawer for phone chargers. A handyman can easily add an electrical outlet near your Destination Station.

Sometimes people have even built in areas for this purpose. Entryway and mudroom pieces that you find online may inspire you, and you can design a customized station for your family's needs. Any cabinet maker or carpenter should be able to make something very attractive for you using beadboard and some cool hooks!

Tried and True Products for Good Measure:

- **Mudroom furniture:** There are a few pieces of furniture we've found in catalogs that are great for this purpose. Search online for "mudroom" and "entryway" furniture. L.L. Bean and Pottery Barn have some good pieces, as do other companies.

- **Driinn phone charger holders:** We sell these nifty gadgets in our online store at ClutterDiet.com. They are plastic holders that provide a place to wind up extra cords and cables as well as a "shelf" for your phone or iPod to rest.

Donation Station

Ingredients for Success:

A good Donation Station is located in a closet, a spot in the garage, or just an out-of-the-way corner—whatever works for you and your family to be able to set aside items you've decided you no longer need. The purpose is to have a place to corral all of those items, once you have made the decision to donate them, giving you less chance of getting them mixed back into your stuff again! Keep some containers you don't mind giving away there, like paper grocery or shopping bags or boxes. Don't make the mistake of putting items in your nice plastic bins, because you probably won't get them back!

A Pinch of This and a Dash of That:

Go to our Free Tips page at www.clutterdiet.com/freetips for our Itemized Donations List form. You may want to have one of these forms handy at this station if you like taking tax deductions for your charitable donations. Include a pen to write items down as you put them there.

Tried and True Products for Good Measure:

- **ItsDeductibleOnline.com:** This web application is now free from Intuit, the makers of Quicken and TurboTax software. It allows you to assign values easily to the household items you are donating. It takes only a few minutes, and it shows your tax savings total in real time as you amass your list of donations. It's always amazing to me how much people underestimate the value of their donated items.

- **Money For Your Used Clothing booklet:** This information is in booklet form, similar to what you would find on ItsDeductible.com. This booklet is available for purchase at www.MFYUC.com and includes more than 700 household items with their proper valuations. The company guarantees you will save $250 on your income taxes by using this book, or your money back!

Education Station

Ingredients for Success:

The Education Station is where you set up a comfortable environment for your children to study and complete their homework assignments. Depending upon your home's configuration, you may want to set this up in a child's bedroom, a common hallway or desk area, or even at the kitchen table. Here's what you'll need:

- A smooth, flat surface, preferably a desk, where the kids can do their work
- Plenty of age-appropriate school supplies
- Blank paper
- Reference sources such as a dictionary, a thesaurus, and an atlas or map
- A computer would be ideal for word processing and research, along with a printer

A Pinch of This and a Dash of That:

If this station is in an area that is often used for other functions, like the kitchen table, create a storage area nearby to contain needed supplies using portable storage options like caddies with handles. These containers are easier to take in and out of the storage area, so you can quickly clean up the kitchen table or other common area for the next use.

If you are deliberating buying a second computer for your home, or if you are replacing the main household computer, strongly consider a notebook instead of a desktop. They use less energy, take up less space, and provide much more versatility and flexibility in how and where they are used.

Set up a Limiting Container, like a basket or tray, for your children's papers. When it's full, that is your cue to go through them. This way you can collect papers in a controlled manner and keep them pared down in volume.

Tried and True Products for Good Measure:

- If you have trouble with limiting the kids' time on the computer, try software like ComputerTime, found at SoftwareTime.com. It provides each child with his or her own login and time limits.

Family Rooms/Playrooms

Ingredients for Success:

Whether you call it a playroom, family room or living room, this place of community in the home is where your family and guests congregate to talk, relax, play and read. Here are the major functions of the family room or playroom:

- Watching movies/TV and Gaming (DVDs, VHS tapes, video game consoles and other media, entertainment center/home theater components, remote controls)
- Listening to music (CDs, stereo components)
- Storing toys/Maintaining a Play Area (toys, games, and storage for them)
- Reading (bookshelves, books, magazines, magazine racks and baskets)
- Relaxing and Entertaining (fireplace tools, matches, blankets, barware, napkins, coasters)

Movies/TV, Gaming, and Music:

To organize the various types of media, divide up your collections by media types—separate the VHS tapes from the DVDs, video games, music CDs, home movies and other formats.

If you have children, your next task may well be to match up all of the cases with the correct contents. Make a pile of "orphan" DVDs, CDs, or tapes, and another pile of "orphan" cases, until you start recognizing matches and putting them together. At the end you're highly likely to end up with a few leftovers. Use plain CD jewel cases to hold orphan CDs and DVDs, and you can label VHS tape orphans on the spine with a metallic Sharpie® marker.

Decide how important it is to you to keep CD and DVD cases. It is efficient storage for CDs and DVDs to keep them in a "wallet" with sleeves, which you can get at any office supply or discount store. CD wallets hold 100-plus CDs in only a few inches of shelf space, as opposed to approximately 30 jewel cases per FOOT of shelf space. Sometimes this idea is frightening to movie and music enthusiasts, so no problem, keep the cases. It's just a suggestion—but it does really save space if you can bear parting with the cases. One compromise is saving the cases in a "D" location where you have more room, and using the wallet idea for the "A" or "B" location where you are actually using the disks.

Whether or not you use the wallet idea, think of sorting your media a few different ways. If you are really a "genre" person who likes thinking of your movies and music by category (action, comedy, horror, classical, jazz, etc.), create one section (or one wallet) per genre, then store them within that category alphabetically by title. If you're using a wallet, leave a few spaces between each letter for new ones, and do NOT worry about doing it perfectly! It takes more effort and time to alphabetize it perfectly than to alphabetize them roughly and flip through a few pages when you're looking for one.

You may want to have two sets of media—grownup movies and music, and kids' movies and music. This is probably realistic for most families.

Go roughly alphabetical by title from there if that is helpful and realistic for your situation. Obviously if kids are grabbing for their movies, the alphabetizing is not going to stick, so just do your best to keep the movies corralled in one centralized area. Be realistic with yourself on this one—it can be a losing battle!

Home movies are obviously things we want to save. If your home movies are on tape, you might look into transferring them to digital media in order to save space and provide a more reliable medium. Find a local service to do this by looking in your Yellow Pages under "Video Production Services." Tape formats deteriorate over time, and digital methods last a little longer and stay true with their color, etc. If you have time (and a box of tissues), look through the movies to see if there are tapes you can discard. If someone grabbed a camera and filmed two minutes of a blurry, unspecified person on a water slide, and there's nothing else on the tape, is that worth saving? Once you have determined which home movies you will keep, decide how often they will be viewed, as this will determine whether you store them in your main media container or keep them tucked away in a memories container in a "C" location.

If you need a new storage piece to hold your media collection, choosing one will depend on not only the number of categories and items that you have in your collection, but also whether you want closed or open storage. Closed storage is more aesthetically pleasing to those who are concerned about interior decorating, and closed doors also prevent the containers from getting dusty. But if you watch movies quite often, and there has been a pattern of borrowers not returning the movies to their homes, you might opt for open shelving. Not having doors in the way will make the "drop-off" area more accessible.

After organizing your media, label the shelves with the categories you have chosen to use, such as by genre (Action shelf, Romance shelf, Home Movie shelf) or alphabetically (A-F, G-L, M-Z). This will help everyone remember which movies belong where. If there are other media players located in the house, establish a rule that the person watching the movie must return it to the proper storage unit before going to bed, or arrange for a cleanup time once a week by those who have used the movies.

Once you run out of room in your media storage unit or shelves, consider using the "one in, one out" rule. You must decide which movie to remove, and part with it before placing a new one in there. That's a good rule for anywhere, by the way!

Toy Storage/Play Area:

Do not use a big gaping toy box. This method of storage is overwhelming and makes things difficult to find. Consequently the contents get dumped out altogether or rooted through. A better choice is using several smaller containers and grouping toys by type if possible.

Most toys are not well-stored in the original boxes they came in from the store. With a few exceptions, these boxes are designed to ship and sell the toys, not store them. It's usually better to cut a picture of the toy off the box and tape it to a new container with clear packing tape.

Use pictures for labeling if kids do not read yet. A combination of words and pictures is ideal. It's easy to find pictures of your toys on Google Images, or just cut them off the original box as described above.

Remember that kids are not going to organize on their own! Even if you organize their toys perfectly, children will still need to be encouraged to pick them up every single day, maybe until they leave home! That's just how kids are, unless you have an exceptional one.

Use open containers without lids when possible. Lids make it more difficult for children to put things away, as there is one additional step involved. Sometimes lids are needed to stack containers, but open, labeled baskets are the easiest for putting things back where they belong.

Keep things at their level. For safety reasons and for ease of use, make sure you look at the room from "kid level" and optimize the storage for them.

Use baskets throughout the house to collect strays. Kids want to follow Mommy or Daddy around, so they take their toys around the house. Keep a medium-sized basket near the door in each room to collect toys, and regularly take these baskets back to the centralized toy storage area that you use (whether a playroom, child's bedroom, or other place).

Reading:

To organize magazines and other periodicals, first centralize all of your reading material. Take a hard look at your subscriptions, and be realistic about whether you truly have time for these publications. Get gutsy and unsubscribe to something—it will feel really good not to see it in the pile anymore. If you haven't read it for three months, cancel the subscription. You can always buy magazines at the newsstand if you really want a specific issue, and you can usually read them online, too. The likelihood of your ever getting a block of spare time to read those older magazines is extremely small.

We recommend having at least one reading basket, located where you do most of your reading. You may want to separate the material into Business,

Personal and Catalogs (these are the most common categories). You might even need to separate your reading material into "A" reading (must read) and "B" reading (read if you can). In our experience, there is no "C" or "D" reading—nobody has time.

Each of your reading baskets can have a set of tools, ideally contained in a pouch or other small container:

- Highlighter pen
- Sticky notes and flags
- Pen or pencil
- Clipping blade or scissors
- Small stapler and staples
- Book weight
- Favorite bookmarks

For bookshelves, first focus on pulling out books you do not want to keep anymore, or those that need to be returned to someone else. You can sell books at a local used bookstore, sell them on eBay, or donate them to either a library or another charity of your choice. If you ever need them again, you can usually check them out at the library yourself or possibly even get the information online.

Next, re-arrange and put away extraneous items that have also ended up on the shelves. If you wish, arrange your books by category or subjects that make sense to you.

If you have more time, categorize your books more thoroughly and arrange them around some bookends and small decorative objects. It always looks nice to group books in sections and then place some kind of meaningful knickknacks here and there to add interest rather than having several solid rows of books.

A Pinch of This and a Dash of That:

If you have a lot of older media, are you really using it on a regular basis? Since many U.S. households now use DVD players, your VHS tapes may be obsolete. Do you still have your VCR connected to your television? If so, it makes sense to keep your VHS tapes, but if you no longer have a player for them, consider donating or disposing of them. If you have a few favorite VHS tapes but they just aren't used very often, put them into less accessible "C" storage that is climate-controlled. When you are sorting through your older media, make sure you have a pen and paper to make note of any items you'd like to replace by purchasing newer versions.

Rotate toys periodically. You can have a couple of boxes stored out of sight where you keep things the children have not been interested in for a while. You can use our member area's Reminder System or your own calendar to remind yourself to switch out the toys—monthly or every other month as you prefer. It's really fun for the kids to see things with fresh eyes and appreciate their things all over again. And if they don't appreciate them when they haven't seen them for a while, that can be a clue that it's time to donate those toys.

Go through toys with your child before birthdays and holidays. Behave as if you have limited space for the toys and you have to get rid of the old to make room for the new. Encourage the children to think of others. Have a Donation Station always available for kids to put toys when they have decided they are tired of them, and educate them (in an age-appropriate way) about children who may not be as fortunate as they are.

Avoid purchasing toys with lots of pieces and parts. At one point in our child-rearing years, we had Legos out the proverbial wazoo. Excessive pieces may be somewhat unavoidable, but do think about this when you are buying something like a big animal zoo play set. There may be a less clutter-prone alternative!

Tried and True Products for Good Measure:

- **Media storage units:** Since it really comes down to a matter of personal taste, and we can't possibly describe all of the available products, we recommend browsing Organize.com and other stores online for "media storage." Mainstream entertainment system furniture is also getting better all the time for providing media storage.

- **Reading accessories, shelving, and furniture:** Levenger is my favorite catalog for all things having to do with reading. They also have some creative office supplies and time management tools.

- **GameSavers:** If you have board game boxes that have fallen apart, you will appreciate this product. I always wish the game manufacturers would make it easier to store the little pieces and cards, and these plastic replacement boxes make everything work better for your Candy Land or Monopoly or other game storage. Available at the Container Store.

- **"Universal System Selector":** Available online from GameStop.com, this switching console allows you to move easily between various video game consoles. If you own more than one console, like a Wii and a Playstation, you can relate to the difficulty of hooking up wires to the back of the television when you want to play a different game, and this product eliminates that problem.

Garages/ Attics/ Basements

Ingredients for Success:

Garages, attics and basements are often the "Final Frontier" of clutter, the catch-all space for the overflow from the home. There are many functions and zones that may apply for these types of storage spaces. Here is a list of a few to get you started:

- Space for parking cars
- Bikes and kids' toys
- Automotive care/car washing
- Tools/workbench/hardware
- Pet care
- Trash and recycling
- Camping gear
- Swimming gear or pool toys
- Lawn furniture/spectator chairs
- Gardening and lawn care equipment and supplies
- Sports equipment/golf/fishing gear
- "C" storage (holiday decorations and memorabilia)
- "D" storage (tax records, spare furniture)

These spaces can usually be classified as a "Clutter Cemetery" as we discussed in Chapter 10, and they often are also "Boneless" spaces without any infrastructure.

The big infrastructure question: Shelving or cabinets? In a garage, my strong preference is for cabinets. The reason is simple...where do you enter and leave your home? For many people, it's the garage, so it's the first and last impression you have of your home every day as you come and go. Do you really want to see all that stuff every day, especially if it may not be attractively organized?

Nearly every major city has a company that can install inexpensive garage cabinetry. In my opinion, it does not have to be elaborate or even high quality, because it's just a garage! As long as it looks nice and is sturdy, the inside of the cabinets themselves do not usually need to be of the highest caliber. You can dispense with having backs on the cabinets, and you can get them done with simple particle-board shelving that will hold a lot of weight. Do your homework and get a product with a good warranty, but don't feel pressured to get the creme-de-la-creme of garage cabinets.

Cabinet companies usually do a great job of designing what you need and have a lot of experience with various garage sizes and configurations, so they are a good resource. If they can build the cabinets all the way up to the ceiling, definitely do that. You will find all kinds of "C" items you can put up there. You can also get workbench areas installed if you need a good work surface.

If you want open shelving for a basement or if you prefer that for your garage, you can usually put that up yourself very easily. I recommend using 16 inch deep shelving if possible, not just the standard 11 or 12 inch shelves. There are large items such as coolers that hang over the edge with the more shallow shelves.

While you are going through the Reviewing and Deciding process in a garage, you will probably want to pull everything out on the driveway to sort it. If you have limited time, focus on one shelving unit, one cabinet, or one corner. If you have time to remove everything from the garage, sweep it and clean it well before putting it back in. A leaf blower can actually be handy for this process, especially if you have cobwebs and leaves in the corners and if you have windows with blinds in your garage. (Wear a mask!)

If the most prominent function of your space is storage, you might want to catalog your storage with an inventory of some kind. Accomplish this indexing by box, by shelf or by general area. You can use Excel spread-sheets or a simple table, even handwritten. Label each box with a number and list the contents by row in your table, or number each shelf and list the contents that way. You can also refer to the walls in your room as Wall A, Wall B, Wall C and Wall D, and generally describe what is stored against each wall. This wall approach might be the best one for an attic situation where you don't have shelving. Keep this storage inventory information in your files or your Family Binder (see our *Communication Station* recipe pages for information on setting up a Family Binder).

A Pinch of This and a Dash of That:

Set up a "parking space" for bikes with electrical tape to show kids where to keep their bikes. Use different colors for multiple bikes.

If your garage has been "let go" for quite some time, you may need to reserve an entire day or possibly even two or more to handle the entire project. If you have been collecting stuff in your garage for 20 years, you will be facing a serious project. We would highly recommend finding a Professional Organizer locally for a project of that magnitude, but if you are not able to do that, try buying your friends some pizza and hoping for the best! You may need to use some tarps to cover piles of items if they need to be left out overnight. Consider the weather in this project, and you may need to call a junk-hauling company or rent a trash container.

If you are storing memorabilia, make sure you are protecting it against excess moisture and extreme climate conditions. Make sure your storage containers are acid-free and won't promote fading and deterioration of photographs. You may even want to consider hiring a scanning service to archive these materials for you digitally. Search online for your city name plus "photo scanning."

The Clutter Diet

Tried and True Products for Good Measure:

- *Organize Your Garage In No Time:* If you are serious about your garage, I highly recommend this book by my dear friend and colleague, Barry Izsak. It is the definitive guide to organizing your garage, with great tips and ideas that will help tremendously if you are undertaking this as a major project.

- **Ceiling storage units:** Installing these units on the ceiling of your garage is like getting an extra attic! They can sometimes be placed above garage doors, so they almost disappear. The most well-known do-it-yourself brands are Onrax and Hyloft, but there are many companies now that have other options and they will come to your home to measure and install them for you. Search online for the name of your city plus "overhead garage storage."

- **Tote Trac:** These storage systems are also for the ceiling but are more versatile than the racks mentioned above. The tracks can be used with your own plastic storage bins and configured in many different ways. See their website at ToteTrac.com for ideas.

- **Bike hoists:** I like the Racor Ceiling-Mounted Bike Lift, available at Amazon.com and many other online and retail stores. It easily lifts your bicycle up to the ceiling and has a safety catch to keep it from falling if you let go while pulling the ropes.

- **Gravity bike racks:** Racor also makes a gravity-based bike rack that holds two bikes and does not require installation to the wall. These are available at local hardware stores, Organize.com, and StacksAndStacks.com.

- **Metal "Metro" shelving:** Your favorite wholesale store or home center probably carries the sturdy chrome "restaurant rack" shelving that holds a lot of weight. These racks are a great option if you need shelving you can take with you when you move.

- **The ultimate garage systems:** There are some exciting and good-looking new options for garages nowadays, and the garage renovation industry is really taking off. You can get the chrome, car-racing look with Gladiator GarageWorks products available from your local home center, and you can find any number of different garage systems available depending upon where you live. Some of the popular options are "GarageTek" and "Premier Garage." These systems look fantastic, but you can potentially spend a LOT of money on them. Before you have a company come to give you an estimate, make sure their services are within your budget before getting into an awkward situation.

- **Garage flooring options:** I personally have used an epoxy flooring kit from our local home center, and we are very happy with the results. You can have garage companies do this for you, and they use a higher-quality epoxy coating. Other options include interlocking tiles and roll-out mats.

Gift and Shipping Station

Ingredients for Success:

You may not have a permanent station set up for gifts and shipping, but at least gather all of these items together in a bin or drawer for easy retrieval when you need them.

Below is a checklist of the major elements of a gift wrapping station. In addition to the items listed below, you'll need a flat surface to do your wrapping and taping. You may want to have all the items in one closet, or you may want to store them in convenient containers under a bed or elsewhere.

- **Scissors:** Have a dedicated pair here instead of bringing them from somewhere else to use each time.

- **Tape dispenser and tape refills:** It's much better to have a heavy, desktop dispenser so you can use just one hand to get a piece of tape. Some people also like double-sided tape.

- **Gift wrap:** Either in rolls or folded pieces. Try to purchase generic wraps that can be used for many different occasions. For example, instead of buying wedding wrap with bells on it, buy a solid spring color and use it for baby gifts too.

- **Gift bags:** Categorize by occasion, such as birthday, holiday, graduation/baby/wedding and all-purpose. Use one gift bag for each category to contain all of the other bags.

- **Tissue paper:** Keep a large quantity of plain white because it goes with everything.

- **Ribbons:** You can dispense ribbons on a roll using a dowel rod to hang them up, if you are handy. Often we just keep them upright on their sides inside a bin or drawer so we can see and grab them easily.

- **Bows:** Keep these in a crush-proof container. Give yourself a limit on bows—especially if you like to re-use them.

- **Gift tags:** "To" and "From" labels establish ownership and avoid confusion. It's smart to have some plain, all-occasion tags as well as holiday ones.

- **Pens and markers:** Use these for labeling gift tags and writing other notes during this process.

- **Sticky notes:** For temporary labeling of gifts. I like the new extra-sticky ones that don't fall off.

- **Extra-large gift bags:** These giant sacks are available for wrapping oversize gifts like a child's bike or beanbag chair. Good to have one or two of these around when you need them.

- **Extra gifts:** Sometimes we call this the "gift shelf," but you can keep these together in a bin or another place that makes sense for you. If you find little hostess gifts and child birthday gifts that are available and that you know will be appropriate for someone, buy them in advance, store them here and you'll always be ready for the next occasion. Give yourself a limit on these gifts, as some people tend to buy too many and never use them.

- **Boxes:** Just a few. Don't go crazy! The collapsible shirt boxes like department stores use are great, since they store well in smaller spaces. If you can break them down, you will be able to store boxes much more efficiently. Keep only a few jewelry boxes and some small, medium and large boxes for wrapping, maybe two or three of each size at the most. Usually gifts come with their own boxes, especially if you ask for one at the store.

A few extra items are great for shipping:

- **Scissors:** Have a dedicated pair here if you don't already.

- **Tape gun:** Use clear packing tape refills. I highly recommend getting a proper tape gun instead of trying to use your teeth or scissors. A tape gun is relatively inexpensive and you can use it primarily with only one hand.

- **Free boxes from US Postal Service:** Stock up on Flat Rate Priority Mail envelopes and Flat Rate Priority Mail boxes. You don't even need to know how much they weigh—it's just a flat amount to mail them. So convenient! You can get all the boxes you want delivered right to your house for absolutely no charge from USPS.com.

- **Stamps:** I like buying a whole roll of stamps. It's such a good idea to have them ready when you need them instead of getting a few at a time. You can buy stamps of any kind online.

- **Shipping scale:** If you have a shipping scale, or at least a smaller postal scale, you may be able to avoid a trip to the post office. It really is worth having if you do a lot of shipping.

- **Packing material:** Use a trash bag as a container to recycle packing material that you receive yourself. Those puffy "air bags" are great, along with Styrofoam peanuts, bubble wrap, etc. Limit yourself to one bagful unless you do an extraordinary amount of shipping. If you are cramped for space, you can always use crumpled newspapers or plastic grocery sacks for this purpose. You'll likely have those around when you need them.

- **Permanent markers:** Sharpie® and Marks-A-Lot® markers are both great.

- **Envelopes:** Gather up various sizes, bubble wrap ones, regular ones and Priority Mail ones. It's best to store these in a vertical sorter.

- **Return address labels:** It's really smart to buy them in quantity on a roll. You can find them online inexpensively at places like CurrentLabels.com, ArtisticLabels.com and SuperiorLabels.com.

A Pinch of This and a Dash of That:

A tall trash can works perfectly well for holding rolls of wrapping paper and it can sit right inside your closet door. There is no need to purchase special upright gift wrap containers unless you really like them or need to have a lid on them.

When I was growing up, my grandmother put up a card table in her guest bedroom and left it out for the whole holiday season for all of us to come over and wrap gifts whenever it was convenient. All gift wrap was out and ready, with ribbons and bows and tape mostly purchased on sale right after Christmas the year before. It was such a great idea, especially since all of the wrapped gifts ended up under her tree where we held our celebration. We just wrapped them and left them there conveniently.

Arrange a free package pickup from the U.S. Postal Service website when you use Priority or Express Mail and pay for it with their online printable postage. I seldom, if ever, have to go to the post office anymore, because my packages are picked up from my front porch! The postal services's online postage is actually less expensive than the regular price, and you can print it from any printer and tape the shipping label onto your package.

Tried and True Products for Good Measure:

- **Elfa gift wrap carts:** If you want to invest in a great solution that stores inside a closet and rolls out when you need it, the Container Store's Elfa gift wrap carts are really wonderful. You'll even have a work surface on the top of the cart.

- **Under-bed wrap containers:** Flat containers that slide easily from under the bed are a great, inexpensive solution for wraps and bows.

- **Dymo Labelwriter Twin Turbo printer:** If you do a lot of shipping, this label printer is terrific because you can have both postage and shipping labels simultaneously ready for printing. The printer comes with free set-up for buying postage online and printing your own stamps.

Kitchens

Ingredients for Success:

Along with your normal organizing toolkit, you'll want to have cleaning cloths to wash off the shelves and possibly a broom and dustpan. Make sure you have lots of heavy-duty trash bags! You'll be surprised how much trash you can generate with all of the food packaging you'll likely discard.

The four F's are probably more important in the kitchen than anywhere else in the house: **F**eatures, **F**low, **F**unction and **F**requency.

The fixed elements of your kitchen, the **Features**, are likely difficult to move without a major renovation. Considering the **Flow** between them is crucial to the way you strategize placement of your items. The "Work Triangle" is the relationship of your movement between the sink, stove and refrigerator. Strategize your placement of food preparation tools, cooking utensils, and food storage containers with these three features in mind to minimize the steps required for preparation and cleanup.

Here are the main functions occurring within a kitchen:

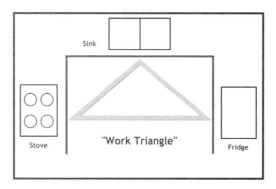

- **Washing and Cleaning:** dishes, food, hands, appliances, surfaces
- **Food Preparation:** chopping, measuring, slicing, mixing, blending
- **Baking:** using mixer, specific ingredients, specific tools
- **Cooking:** baking, boiling, frying, roasting, broiling
- **Serving:** dishes, utensils, accessories
- **Food Storage:** plastic storage containers, foils, wraps
- **Pantry:** cereals, dry goods, rice & beans, soups, beverages, etc.

And here are some optional functions to consider:

- **Lunch Making Center:** lunch boxes, thermal containers, plastic utensils
- **Coffee/Beverage Center:** mugs, tea, sweeteners, filters, coffee—near water source (Okay, it's a "Caffeination Station")
- **Children's Snack Center:** accessible items for them to help themselves to snacks and easy breakfasts, with non-breakable dishware and cups and easy snack foods such as cereal, granola bars and dried fruit.

Your kitchen probably has more "gear" than any other room in the house, so **Frequency is essential to consider.** Use the A-B-C-D prioritizing method to think about your gadgets and gizmos and make sure they are assigned spaces that correspond with the reality of how you use them and how often.

Your pantry area, whether it's one small cabinet or an entire closet, is one of the best areas to give your attention. Remember that visibility is key—you can't cook it and eat it if you can't see it and know you have it! Here are some of the most common categories for reviewing and sorting your pantry items:

- Bread & Buns
- Cereal
- Sauces
- Syrup and Honey
- Jams & Jellies
- Canned Tomatoes
- Pasta
- Beans & Rice
- Beverages
- Snacks
- Chips
- Baking Mixes
- Flour & Sugar
- Canned Vegetables
- Canned Beans
- Canned Fruit
- Dried Fruit & Nuts
- Spices
- Crackers

A Pinch of This and a Dash of That:

Use baskets or bins as drawers. You can get baskets that are the depth of the shelf, load them up, and then pull them out like a drawer to get things in and out. Make sure you label the baskets so you will have visibility to what's in there. Small items like individual oatmeal packets, snack bars and boxes of raisins are especially better stored in bins to corral them effectively.

People are often surprised that I do NOT believe in buying big sets of matching pantry containers. It may look neat, but transferring every cracker and marshmallow into containers is not how I would like to spend my time. Often you can't fit all of it into the container and still end up with the remainder in the original bag anyway. In addition, my children eat things up so quickly that it would hardly be worth the effort!

Stacking and nesting items like bowls, plasticware, and pots and pans are great ways to save space in drawers and cabinets. If you have nonstick pans that are sensitive to being scratched, place a coffee filter, paper towel or a piece of cut felt between them.

Do you really need a corn butterer, potato baker or cookie press? How about a "Hello Kitty" waffle maker? Kitchen gadgets hit us where it hurts. We aspire to be amazing cooks like the ones we see on TV, and buying these gadgets gets us one mental step closer to being like Rachael Ray or the Iron Chefs. For just five or 10 dollars, you too can be a chef extraordinaire! Never mind that you actually have to use the gadgets! When is the last time you garnished something, anyway?

There are a certain number of expected and useful gadgets and small appliances in a kitchen: a potato peeler, a can opener, a juicer, and even an apple slicer are all things you would probably use and enjoy. But there are other things many of us have bought on impulse that we will never use.

There are really three kinds of gadgets and tools:

- Preparation tools (knives, potato peelers, food processors)
- Cooking tools (spatulas, whisks, steamers)
- Serving tools (serving tongs, corn cob holders)

It helps to segregate them according to these functions and then place them where they are best used (prep tools near the sink and trash, cooking tools by the stove, and serving tools near the table).

Plastic food containers are often a jumbled mess. In the controversial debate between storing lids separately or together with their containers, I fall in the "separately" camp. I like nesting and stacking the containers of similar shapes and storing the lids together in a bin so that you can flip through them and choose one easily. Did you know that major storage brands usually code their lids and containers with a single letter or number (like "A" or "8") stamped into the bottom? You can use this code to match them up.

Don't forget that refrigerators can also be organized. Do you serve toast in the mornings or biscuits? Why not get a bin and put all of your jellies and jams in there and carry the bin to the table, instead of juggling an armful of various jars? You can assign homes to items—more than just the milk jug. The main issue in organizing refrigerators is maintenance. You need to make sure that there is not spoiled food that will get smelly or make people sick and you've got to make room for the new stuff to come in. The easiest way to maintain the fridge is to "hook your habit" to the day before your trash is picked up. If your trash day is Wednesday, our members can set an e-mail reminder in our Reminder System to do a quick clean-out of the refrigerator on Tuesdays. This way any smelly food will get thrown out and taken away, and it will keep things moving out regularly. It only takes five minutes.

It's official: It's okay to have a junk drawer! Really! Having one does not mean that you are not organized. There are always "doo-dads" in every home that nobody knows where to store. In my junk drawer, we have those little packets of floral food, the small pieces to our holiday light timers, an extra pair of scissors, some glue sticks, and some little round black magnets (among other things). The reason it works is that the things in the drawer are limited, and they are visible and easy to find due to the use of drawer dividers. Most discount stores now sell good "junk drawer dividers" specifically made for this purpose, with lots of little compartments and a top sliding tray. Dividers are the key to making this work.

What NOT to do with a junk drawer: Don't keep things in there that have a home somewhere else, don't keep things that you have not used in more than a year or two, and don't pile too much in the drawer so that you cannot see what's in it. Keep only enough in there so that it's all visible.

Tried and True Products for Good Measure:

- **Drawer dividers:** The common, white, plastic, interlocking drawer dividers that are found in any discount store are often the best. You may even find them sold in a packaged assortment. For utensils I highly recommend spending a little extra money to get the specialty utensil dividers that have large, expandable compartments. These are found at major housewares stores like Bed Bath & Beyond and online at Organize.com. Always measure drawers before purchasing.

- **Museum Putty:** When you use drawer dividers, they may slide around when you open and close the drawers. You can store small "C" or "D" items at the backs of the drawers to help push the dividers to the front, but we like using a tiny dab of Museum Putty to keep them from sliding at all. We started selling this putty in our online store because we like it so much (ClutterDiet.com). We also use it for keeping displayed items stable on shelves.

- **Helper shelves:** Made of laminate, wood, metal or plastic, these little shelves are terrific for using wasted vertical space where you are otherwise unable to add an actual shelf. I love using these for coffee mugs and pantry items to add another layer of shelving quickly and inexpensively. These are sold in major discount stores and a better selection is found in specialty housewares stores.

- **Turntables/Lazy Susans:** Turntables allow you to spin things around and make what was once behind everything now be in the front. Sometimes the standard 10" ones found in any discount store are not enough, and you can buy larger ones at specialty kitchen stores. I especially love turntables for spices.

- **Sterilite #1622 bins:** We like these open bins because they fit on a standard shelf and will still allow cabinet doors to close, and they are quite inexpensive. You'll find these at most major discount stores.

- **Our SpaceScaping® Kitchen Organizing System:** I invented this process for organizing a kitchen when we move clients into a new home, but you could certainly use the same method to reorganize an existing kitchen or even plan a renovation. All of the common categories of kitchen items are printed onto 60 repositionable labels. We tested many adhesives to find one that would not harm cabinets and would pull off quickly and easily as you change your mind during the process. You place the labels on the front of the cabinets to strategize placement of your items before you start moving things around, and the labels guide you as you put things into place. You avoid breakage of delicate glassware because you're not moving it around excessively, while making sure that everything has a home before you start physically moving things. Leave the labels up temporarily as your family gets accustomed to the new arrangement, preventing needless questions from everyone and the endless slamming of doors and drawers. Some people move the labels to the inside of the cabinet doors afterward to remind them of the purpose of the cabinet, or you can simply throw them away. We sell these sets of labels on our website at ClutterDiet.com.

- **Pot racks:** These are both attractive and functional in a kitchen, and they really add warmth, too. Whether ceiling or wall mounted, pot racks are one of the best ways to free up cabinet space in your kitchen. Search for them online and at local specialty stores.

- **"Lid Maid" lid holder:** We like keeping lids separate from pots and pans. This product installs quickly and easily with just a screwdriver. It slides in and out and holds many lids in just a couple of inches of space. Available at Organize.com, the Container Store, and other online stores.

- **Foil and wrap holders:** These are plastic caddies that attach with screws to a wall or the back of a cabinet door, and they are shaped to hold boxes of foil, plastic wrap, and plastic bags. Available almost anywhere.

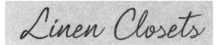

Ingredients for Success:

Start organizing your linens in the main linen closet, or if there is not a centralized location, start in one bathroom and work your way around to the others. Sort through your towels, sheets and blankets, putting the "keepers" together in categories by type, size and then by location. For example, you'll put all the sheets together; then categorize them by King, Queen or Twin; then sort them according to where they need to be stored.

Sheets

Any bed requires only two sets of sheets—one to wash, and one to "wear." Some people might have different sheet fabrics for winter as well. But any more than this is probably a drain on limited space. If you are confused about the sizes of folded sheets, use a laundry marker to mark a lower corner of the sheet with a "K," "Q," or "T." You can then tell the size without unfolding them completely.

Towels

Each person needs to have at least two sets of a bath towel, washcloth and hand towel. Families vary on how often people use a new towel, so you be the judge of this, but do think about whether you have too many. People usually have favorite towels they always grab first and they never use the others.

Blankets, Quilts, and Comforters

The correct quantity for blankets is subjective, but if you don't use them, bulky blankets are a big waste of space. Consider that most families have their favorite blankets and the rest are just extra volume.

Once you've sorted your items, store them closest to their point-of-use, or if you have a large centralized closet, store them there together. Most people have few problems storing their linens once they've pared them down to what they actually use and need.

A Pinch of This and a Dash of That:

The most common issue we see with linens is that there are simply too many. As you start sorting, remember to put aside for donation anything you're not using and discard anything that is faded, torn or stained (see our definitions of trash in Chapter 9).

Please don't save the "good towels" just for guests! You deserve to have nice linens for your own daily use.

Fold your items properly to help your linen closet stay organized. It doesn't matter so much *how* you fold them as long as you fold similar items consistently the same way. This habit allows you to create neat stacks that won't fall over as easily.

Get Your Greens

Recycling Rags: You may want to reuse your older, worn linens as cleaning rags. And if you go camping or fishing often or have a vacation home, save some of the less-than-ideal linens for those uses. We recommend that you separate them from your normal items so they do not get mixed back into regular use. You can use a labeled bin to store them elsewhere if your linen closet does not have room.

Sometimes these items mistakenly end up back in regular circulation. To avoid confusing which items are rags, tear them into smaller pieces. Another differentiating method is to use permanent laundry markers to mark a big "X" on them.

When buying towels in the future, consider color-coding the towels to your bathrooms. Only the blue towels go in the kids' bathroom, the burgundy ones in the master, and so on. Another simplifying choice is to go "hotel-style," using all white for everyone! Think about which system would make it easier for your family to put away the laundry.

If you have heirloom quilts, make sure you're not keeping them in plastic, as quilts need to breathe. You can buy special cloth quilt covers at the Container Store and other specialty retailers. Consider displaying these instead of keeping them hidden away.

Some people have enough room in their linen closets to store extra bathroom items and toilet paper. Make sure you're thinking about frequency of use (A, B, C, D items) and how to best prioritize where you put these types of items.

Tried and True Products for Good Measure:

- **Under sink shelving units:** See our recipe pages on Bathrooms for a further description of the under sink shelving that we like using to maximize bathroom cabinet space. This may be a good place for you to keep some towels and washcloths.
- **Shelf dividers:** These dividers are made of acrylic or chrome, and they slide onto your shelves to keep stacks from falling over on each other.

This can be useful for sheets and towels in a tight space.

- **Space Bags®:** We like these large zip closure bags for bulky blankets and comforters that are seldom used. They have a vacuum valve for you to get out the excess air, and you use a common household vacuum cleaner to compress the volume dramatically. You can get these at any housewares stores, such as Bed Bath & Beyond.

Utility Rooms

Ingredients for Success:

Lorie's "Basic Twelve" Functions of the Ideal Laundry Room:

1. Washer/Dryer (obviously)

2. Sorting and Staging Space: Space to sort dirty clothes

3. Folding Space: A flat surface to fold clothes

4. Hanging Space: Space for at least 5-10 hanging clothes

5. Drip Dry Space: For drying lingerie and exercise gear

6. Storage/Shelving: For holding clean clothes and other items

7. Cleaning and Laundry Supplies: All the stuff you need for cleaning

8. Ironing Station: Storage for ironing board, iron and starch

9. Maintenance Supplies: Tools, Light bulbs, batteries

10. "Lonely Socks" place: Drawer or basket for the misfit socks

11. Pocket Items: Place for things found in pockets, loose change

12. Trash Can: For dryer lint and softener sheets, etc.

Think through your laundry room and how it handles these 12 elements. Are there other functions happening in this room that prohibit the essentials from existing? If these basic elements are not happening in the laundry room, where are they happening? For example, do you fold laundry on your couch or dining table? (I do use my dining table; there is nothing wrong with doing that if you don't have folding space. The key is not keeping the laundry on there perpetually.)

A Pinch of This and a Dash of That:

We spend a lot of our time doing laundry, and this area is one of the "hubs" of the home, whether you have a dedicated room for it or just a spot in the garage or basement. Investing time and money to make this area work smoothly is important to the function of your home and will save you a considerable number of hours over the years.

The first thing you want to do when working on the utility room area is make sure you have put away all of the clean clothes and sorted/staged all of the dirty clothes to be washed while you continue to work.

As you are putting things away, remember that if you have small children you may need to be more careful about potential poisons in cleaning supplies, so take the necessary measures to keep things up and away from little hands.

Remember the back of the door for lots of extra storage space! You can find large racks and many other "overdoor" products that solve almost any problem.

Consider reversing the swing of either your washer or your dryer door, if you are able to do so. If you open the washer and need to load wet clothing into the dryer to the right, and the door of the dryer swings from the left, it can block you from easily tossing the clothing into the machine. If the wall connections are not preventing it, you may be able to move the position of the machines themselves to solve this problem.

Tried and True Products for Good Measure:

- **Rolling storage carts:** If you have at least nine inches of space between your washer and dryer, you can use a white plastic rolling cart to gain about six linear feet of storage space. Along with the incredible use of formerly wasted space, these create convenience in that heavy laundry supplies are now stored closer to the washer, resulting in less lifting. This cart is available at ImprovementsCatalog.com and Spacesavers. com, but you may be able to find it in your local housewares stores as well. You'll want to get the white plastic kind, as the metal versions of these carts tend to be "rickety" and wobbly.

- **Simple Division® Garment Organizers:** Typically we use them in closets, but they are great for sorting clothing by family member when you hang up items from the dryer. These dividers can be labeled with each family member's name and placed on the laundry room's hanging rod. Having the clothing grouped by person makes it much easier to grab and put away quickly. Purchase in 12-packs or 50-packs at ClutterDiet.com.

- **Mounted accordion-style drip-drying rack:** If you hang your delicate washables and sports gear to air dry, you can spare yourself from hanging things in the shower or over your stair railings with this space-saving product. The one I like best is from the Container Store (search "Accordion Drying Rack"). It stretches out to hold your clothing and pushes back to the wall when you're not using it.

- **Sorting hampers:** If you have room, you also might do well to purchase a sorting hamper, so that you can stage the next sorted loads of laundry and keep them out of the way. Any major discount store carries these. Labeling the compartments with a string tag or laundry marker is helpful for the family to see where to put each type of clothing—we usually label them "Whites," "Darks," "Delicates" or "Multi-colored" for the in-between clothes.

- **Ironing caddies:** This product mounts on the wall to hang up your ironing board and easily stores your iron and spray starch. I love how it keeps the ironing supplies all together and out of the way. You can find these at any discount store. Take note of whether you have "Y" or "T" style of legs on your ironing board before purchasing. Some caddies will accommodate only one type.

- **Sharpie® Rub-A-Dub® Laundry Markers:** We use these to mark clothing for easier sorting by family member. Available at office supply stores.

- **Overdoor valet hooks:** If you require additional hanging space, there are a number of overdoor options for hooks that hold several hangers. Search for "overdoor" at Organize.com or ContainerStore.com to see many options, and check the laundry aisle at major discount stores.

For expert organizing help online:
Clutter Diet's program at www.clutterdiet.com

For hands-on organizing help in person:
Search the *National Association of Professional Organizers* at www.napo.net

Notes

Chapter 1

[1] Food Marketing Industry Speaks, 2007

[2] Wikipedia list of all breakfast cereals, 386 items, November 2008
http://en.wikipedia.org/wiki/List_of_breakfast_cereals

[3] American Society of Magazine Editors
http://www.magazine.org/ASME/EDITORIAL_TRENDS/1145.aspx

Chapter 5

[4] "Sustainability: The Global Challenge," ZPG Backgrounder, Washington, D.C.,
Zero Population Growth

[5] National Association of Home Builders
http://prudential.starnewsonline.com/default.asp?item=666853

[6] ABC News December 27, 2005
http://abcnews.go.com/GMA/Moms/story?id=1445039

Chapter 6

[7] Economides, Steve and Annette, America's Cheapest Family Gets You Right on the
Money, Three Rivers Press, 2007.

Chapter 20

[8] The American Heritage® New Dictionary of Cultural Literacy, Third Edition.
Houghton Mifflin Company, 2005.

Acknowledgements

To my clients, who made this book possible with your trust in my expertise. Many of you eventually became friends, and I am so grateful for your influence.

To Pete, without whose support, love, encouragement and patience, nothing whatsoever in my career would be possible. We've invested time, money and energy and sacrificed family time and potential income of other kinds to follow this dream. Thank you for believing in me.

To Reese and Mason, for your patience and support as I travel, make you wait too long at the bus stop sometimes and sit in front of my laptop too much. I truly value your ideas and contributions to my business as we talk on the way to school and back. You make me proud every day with your humor, love, compassion and intelligence.

To my family—Memaw, Mom, Dad, Steve, Kelsey, and April—for your support over these many years of ups and downs. Thank you for listening to me and believing in me.

To Susan Sabo, for insisting that I look into internet marketing. Thank you for being one of my closest and dearest friends and colleagues and my longtime "Accountability Partner" since our first conference in 2001.

To Audrey Thomas, my second Accountability Partner and dear friend. Thank you for helping me "finish strong."

To my editor, Lorraine Fisher, for your attention to detail and your ideas that go beyond commas and grammar. Thank you for your help!

To Stacey Kannenberg, for your encouragement in getting this book published. Thank you for your recommendations of resources and for your positive and helpful attitude in everything you do.

To Anne Tiedt, for helping me think big enough to talk to the right people, reach out to the right media outlets, and go for the big time! I am very grateful for our friendship and our work together.

Acknowledgements

To Yvette Clay and Helene Segura, for taking this ride with me and being supportive and encouraging during the time I was developing the Clutter Diet program. You are powerful, strong, smart women with whom I am proud to associate my name and my brand, and am also proud to call my friends.

To all former employees and associates of LivingOrder who each taught me something important in your own way. There were many incredibly good experiences along with a few difficult lessons, and I am thankful for the experiences we had together.

To Geralin Thomas, for being the first organizer on our team outside of LivingOrder and Texas, and for bringing your expertise on Chronic Disorganization to our member community. You are a woman of grace, class, experience and wisdom.

To Jeffrey Peltier, my secret weapon, for going so far above and beyond the call of duty with your help and support of Clutter Diet. I would not have survived the first year of this business without your help. I am forever grateful for your belief in me and my vision.

To Donna Coffelt, for being my trusted graphic designer for this book and so many other products and projects over the years. You are the best!

To the LEOs, especially Linda Rothschild, Vicki Norris, and Barbara Hemphill, for your support and friendship!

To Barry Izsak, for your friendship, encouragement, and leadership in our industry. I am so grateful for you in my life.

To Shawn Kershaw, my talent show partner and friend, who makes every conference memorable. Thank you for your infectious laugh and your intrepid foray into doing our little show.

To my other NAPO friends everywhere:
Any given day I could be talking on the phone with NAPO friends in Georgia, California, Pennsylvania, Washington, Colorado, North Carolina, DC, and many other places. I am immensely fulfilled by my NAPO friendships and thank you for your support of the talent show and our other fun stuff that makes conference a "never miss" event. You are my tribe!

What People Are Saying About
The Clutter Diet's Online Coaching Program

"I have DOZENS of books on cleaning, decluttering, and organizing, and this site is the best thing that I have ever seen! The quick feedback is very rewarding to me and I also get inspired about the efforts others are making. I am not ALONE in my clutter problem!"
–"Catfife," Member

"The Clutter Diet is just what you need to jumpstart organizing your life. It's the next best thing to having an organizer standing next to you!"
– Linda Rothschild, Cross It Off Your List, New York, NY

"This is exactly what I've been needing to get myself more organized and have better habits so I'll have more precious time. Thanks a lot, it's a great website!"
– Melodie, Alberta, Canada

Get affordable, personal help from our team of Professional Organizers… online!

Our innovative program includes:

- **Access to as much help as you need** from our team of experienced Professional Organizers via our message board support.

- **A weekly plan of action** to keep your house and life organized in about 2 hours per week. Each week there is a Main Dish (the main project for the week), 2 Side Dishes (your two smaller projects), a Sensible Snack (a quick task or tip) and a Dessert (the fun reward!).

- **Access to your own personalized e-mail reminder system,** customized for your needs. You can remind yourself of birthdays, regular home maintenance, or other recurring tasks or events! This feature is a tremendous value alone!

- **Access to over 2 hours of easy multimedia tutorials** to help you learn organizing concepts and methods at your own pace.

- **Personal tracking of your progress.** Each week you can "weigh in" to see how many "Clutter-Pounds[SM]" you have lost so far.

- **Automatic 10% member discount** in our online store, along with member specials, surprises, and advanced notice of new offerings.